BANGED UP
ABROAD
HELLHOLE

*We would like to dedicate this book to
our parents for all their love and support*

BANGED UP ABROAD

HELLHOLE

OUR FIGHT TO SURVIVE
SOUTH AMERICA'S DEADLIEST JAIL

JAMES MILES & PAUL LOSEBY

EBURY
PRESS

3 5 7 9 10 8 6 4 2

This edition published 2012
First published in 2011 by Ebury Press, an imprint of Ebury Publishing
A Random House Group company

The Random House Group Limited Reg. No. 954009

Addresses for companies within the Random House Group can be found at
www.randomhouse.co.uk

A CIP catalogue record for this book is available from the British Library

The Random House Group Limited supports The Forest Stewardship
Council (FSC®), the leading international forest certification organisation.
Our books carrying the FSC label are printed on FSC® certified paper.
FSC is the only forest certification scheme endorsed by the leading
environmental organisations, including Greenpeace.
Our paper procurement policy can be found at
www.randomhouse.co.uk/environment

Printed in Great Britain by
Clays Ltd, St Ives plc

ISBN 9780091946791

To buy books by your favourite authors and register for offers visit
www.randomhouse.co.uk

CONTENTS

PROLOGUE

My name is James Miles and I'm a convicted drug smuggler.

That's something that's quite hard to say.

I don't expect or want any sympathy from you. I did the crime, and served the time. I had it coming and took it on the chin. I knew the risks. So did my partner in crime, Paul Loseby. We were just two young dreamers from Leicester until we agreed to try and smuggle ten kilos of cocaine into Britain from Venezuela. I was just eighteen and Paul twenty-one, but our innocence was erased forever by what we saw in some of the world's most brutal jails. And as for Venezuela? We didn't even know where it was. Neither of us had even been abroad before. We didn't even own passports.

I know drugs are wrong and some people might think supplying them is as bad as murder itself. I'm not stupid. But whatever you think of our crime, nobody should have to go through what we experienced.

We served four years in Venezuelan jails: an existence where every minute of every day was lived in abject fear for our lives. For four years, our lives were only worth eighty pence – the price of a bullet in those jails. In fact, scratch that: our lives were worthless, because knives were made from sharpened prison bars, and they were free.

Humans are at the top of the food chain, not just because we're the cleverest beings on Earth, but because we are the most ruthless. During my time in the jails, I became aware that I was capable of unspeakable acts of violence. I realised that if you treat a man like an animal for long enough, then he becomes one – especially when he is caged. While we were in prison, we both did things we're not proud of. But we did them to survive. It was the law of the jungle. It was do or die.

An old friend we randomly bumped into in a nightclub had been smuggling cocaine, and he set it all up for us. Him and a drug smuggler I'll call the Russian (I won't use his real name, as he told me back then that he'd kill me if we ever grassed him up).

The worst I'd ever done before Venezuela was smoking spliffs and getting involved in a punch-up outside a boozer. I'd never even seen cocaine, let alone taken it or smuggled it. Cocaine was for rich people and the famous, not for ordinary, working-class lads like us. We just wanted to get rich quick, and set ourselves up back home in business.

So we rolled the dice.

And lost.

The Venezuelan attitude to prison is to let the inmates pretty much police themselves. The brutal Venezuelan National Guard – who police the jails – just sit and watch from their gun towers on the perimeter fence of the prison, polishing their machine guns, just putting a bullet through your head if you try to escape.

The police were totally corrupt, completely bent. They were the main artery for guns, drugs and all contraband coming into the jails. The very cops that nicked us were smuggling in every conceivable kind of drug and selling them to inmates. Three kilos of the drugs seized from us went 'missing' while in police custody. You don't have to be a professor to work out what they did with it. Everything had a price and literally everything was for sale. Even life itself.

Everybody carried knives all the time. If you didn't have one, you were dead. It really was as basic as that. But the prisons were also full of machine guns, pistols and even hand grenades. At least five or six men were murdered in any one week in Venezuela's most gruesome jail, Yare. Paul and I spent eighteen months there, so you can do the math on how many deaths we saw during our time; on one night alone in Yare, we witnessed sixty men get massacred in a barbaric prison riot where gunfire was ringing out all night.

It was like we were in the middle of the Gulf War. Men were on fire, desperately trying to climb barbed wire fences to escape rampaging gangs of armed-to-the-teeth murderers. But the guards were just shooting them through the head – they were on the fence, so it was fair game to them. It was open warfare, a total massacre. And what was the cause of this killing spree? The whereabouts of a £1,000 Desert Eagle pistol all the top daddies wanted to own.

It was like the most savage movie you've ever seen, only it was real and, worse, it was happening to us.

I want to tell this story because if it deters even one silly kid, like we were, from drug smuggling, it will have been worth it. The world needs to know about the horrors that go on in Venezuelan jails, and jails like these all over the world, because until people find out, it will never be changed.

We were caught smuggling ten kilos of cocaine out of Venezuela on November 6th, 1996, and we didn't get back to England until December 6th, 2000.

What came in between was the stuff of nightmares.

Paul and I have written this book together, but it's from my point of view. Paul was my rock in jail and found ways to keep himself sane, while I'll be the first to admit that I went completely crazy.

'I could see what was going on from the outside, kid,' Paul said when we talked about doing this book. 'But only you know what was going on inside. And, others need to know that, too.' It's not the easiest story to tell. But it has to be done if Paul and I ever hope to move on. So this is it. This is our story.

CHAPTER 1
FIXED

I often wonder how very different my life might have been if I hadn't gone out to Crystals nightclub, in Leicester, on that fateful night back in October 1996. There might have been a good film on the telly. I might have stayed in with my girlfriend instead. I might have sat there, got stoned and just not bothered to get my arse in gear. But my old school mate, Paul, and I did go out that night, and we ended up in the nightclub at precisely the same moment as the Russian.

And it changed the course of our lives forever.

How did my life come to this?

There was nothing for us in Leicester. I'd left school without any qualifications, and had worked in my uncle's scrap yard for £20 a week, but had got fed up skinning my knuckles taking out alternators at 7 a.m. on dark, freezing-cold mornings, so I was on the dole.

I really should have stuck with my football. I used to be pretty good at it, but I always felt it was more about what my dad, Steve, wanted for me. He'd pumped it into me, would kick me out of bed in the mornings to get me to go to training, and I just got fed up of being bossed about. So, I'd jacked it in, really as a way of rebelling against him. I body-swerved his plan and decided to take my own path.

Along with this, my parents had recently been through a messy split, and my dad was living in Germany. That really took its toll on me. I felt abandoned, isolated and hurt. And with no father figure around, I became pretty uncontrollable.

I knew Paul from my schooldays, and we'd share a spliff together while playing computer games at a mate's house when we couldn't afford to go out, which was pretty much all the time.

Life was shit. There were no jobs and no prospects. We'd get pissed and stoned, and in the morning, we'd still wake up with no money in our pockets. It would be pissing down with rain and there'd be no way out of the boring hole we were in.

Paul had been in the army, but got discharged from his basic training on medical grounds after twisting one of his bollocks after five weeks. They'd sent him home, and told him if he wanted to be re-admitted to the Forces, he'd have to start the whole training over again. 'Five more weeks of crawling through puddles while some big bastard shouts at you?' he'd said. 'Sod that for a game of soldiers.'

He'd had to go back home and live with his parents, same as me. He'd joined the army to see the world and become a man. But when his chance was taken from him due to sheer bad luck, he was left feeling rejected and foundationless.

Paul had also done various crap jobs like me – in factories and on building sites. We would sit around and talk about how we felt we were both just breaking our backs and existing; living for the weekends when we'd blow all our money on beer, then just start again. We were both rebellious spirits, and were fed up of having to live under the rules and regulations of being at home. We were very much just your average, hormone-filled, bored teenagers. There was nothing remotely out of the ordinary about our lives.

Like millions of other British lads at that time, our heroes were Noel and Liam Gallagher from Oasis. They were working-class boys like us, and they'd made it big. It seemed to us that they'd come from nowhere to being megastars in five minutes. They seemingly hadn't given a toss, but suddenly Oasis were celebrities and millionaires. And they'd done it without any interference from their parents; they'd made it on their own terms.

Paul and I wanted a life like that. But how were we going to get it? And who would give us an opportunity?

*

Crystals was our favourite nightclub and we went there most weekends, as the booze was cheap and you always had a decent chance of getting your leg over. It was pretty much your standard British meat market.

As soon as we walked in that night, a bloke at the bar caught my eye. He was an old mate of ours called Luke, but I hardly recognised the man who stood before me.

I'd last seen Luke in Crystals about four months before. He'd always been a bit of a pikey and looked scruffy, dressing in cheap clobber from Tesco or some-where. But there he was, dressed in an Armani suit and box-fresh Nikes, with plenty of bling jewellery. He'd totally changed the way he looked – he had to be living the high life.

He'd obviously been abroad, as he was tanned and looked healthy; you don't get that working down a scrap yard in Leicester. He was flashing money around at the bar, standing huge rounds of drinks for everybody, and I thought how nice it must be to wake up with money in your pocket, rather than grinding out an existence for pittance in a crap job.

But it wasn't just the money. This new Luke oozed confidence. The way he carried himself; it was like he'd become a celebrity. People wanted to be around him, both blokes and girls. He just had that air about him. Right there on the spot, I knew I wanted a piece of it.

Paul and I nervously shuffled towards him and we got talking.

'You look like you're doing well for yourself, kid,' I said. 'What have you done, robbed a bank?'

'No, you soft sod,' he smiled. And started to tell us his story.

Luke told us how he'd just got back from Venezuela. Apparently it was a country in South America, just below Mexico and Jamaica. I'd never even heard of the place, to be honest. Venezuela? Was that near Vancouver? Like in Canada? We didn't have a clue.

Luke started going on about how he did business for a friend out there, and while he was there stayed in a five-star hotel, complete with a swimming pool surrounded by palm trees and fancy seafood restaurants.

'Have you ever been abroad, Jim?' he asked.

'Never been abroad in my life, mate,' I replied, trying to act cool. But inside, it stung, because my parents had never been able to take me abroad. We lived on an estate. Foreign travel was something other people did.

'You've got to do it, mate,' Luke enthused. 'I've just got back from another trip. I'm telling you, I've been living every lad's dream. Everything's cheap as fuck in Venezuela – even the girls, if you know what I mean! There's a party every night, loads of cheap booze, cheap fags, nights out cost bugger all, there's palm trees every-where and as for the birds … they make this lot in here look like the dogs they are. It's totally mega. Why bother going to Spain where everything's so pricey? Get your arses to Venezuela, mate. Everything's double beautiful, and double cheap. It's fookin' beautiful.'

I looked over at Paul. I could tell he was buying it. Luke was still going on: 'It's a pretty rich country, but most live like it's a third-world country. If you've got money, you can control everything out there. You can live like a king, mate! It's as good as Ibiza, with twenty-four-hour parties, but it's a fraction of the cost.'

I'll admit, I was impressed. Luke had painted a pretty convincing picture, and it all sounded so exotic and faraway.

'How did you afford to get out there, to do all this?' I asked.

'I've been helping a Russian bloke, a business associate of mine, smuggle drugs,' he said. 'I've been smuggling cocaine.'

He came out with it just like that. Of course, we'd heard of cocaine. Oasis took it. To us, cocaine was all Miami, the high life, what famous people did. We knew you snorted it up your nose. But we'd never set eyes on the stuff.

Luke continued. 'Nobody ever gets caught, because everybody's paid off to let you through at the airport. It's all set up so it can't go wrong. I send people over there, so it's all OK-ed in advance.' He swigged his beer. 'It's an organisation, where everything's sorted, everything's protected down to the finest detail. We've got special gateways at the airport so everybody gets through without getting checked.' He grinned. 'The airport officials are all in on it, too. They've got our people's photographs, and they just wave them through. Everything has a price out there – even the police. If you did it, you wouldn't have to worry about a thing, mate.'

It sounded too good to be true, but it also sounded kosher. Luke had done it a couple of times, and he'd told us that mates of his who had done it had got away with it as well. They weren't in jail. In fact, just the opposite; they were living really well.

'How much would we get?' I asked, cutting to the chase.

'You'd get five grand each – cash – for smuggling five kilos each,' he replied.

Five grand? That was more cash than I'd ever had in my life. It seemed like silly money.

I was excited but, of course, I was also scared. Going abroad was daunting enough, but to go abroad for the first time to smuggle drugs? But this would give me a quick and easy way of getting away from my family, to get my own place and make my own way in the world.

I wanted a quick fix. Why work for £20 a week in a dead-end job and scrimp and save for years, when this seemed like the perfect short cut?

Looking back, I'll admit I was completely naive, and I'm not looking for sympathy. But right then, in that nightclub, I was convinced we'd found a secret formula to get minted. My desire for financial stability, my desire to prove I could make it on my own in the world, my greed and a get-rich-quick scheme took over my mind.

I decided I would invest the money in something for the future, like a nice little garage, where I'd repair cars – my family had always been into cars – to set me up in life. Paul wanted to set up a car valet business and five grand would get him going, too.

He and I looked at each other, then nodded. We were in.

'This Russian bloke, how do we find him, then?' I said to Luke.

'That's him over there,' he said, pointing to a man in a flash suit who looked different from everybody else. He was an older guy, and was standing there all relaxed, with a look that said, 'I'm rich – don't fuck with me.' He looked foreign, a bit like Borat, with a moustache and dark hair swept to the side. He was a big guy, and he looked very powerful, and not just physically – he had an aura of power. He wasn't dancing around like everybody else; he had a cool, calm air to him. But there was also menace there. He looked like he had connections to the kind of people who get things done – no matter what it took. It was all pretty intimidating to two young lads. But I've always been a risk-taker, and not for a moment did I feel worried for my own safety.

Looking back, it's obvious that Luke was his gofer, the bloke who would handpick people from the club and then introduce them to him.

Well, we fell for it hook, line and sinker. 'Let's go and meet him,' I said.

And with that, Luke took us over to meet the man that was going to fuck up our lives completely.

A few minutes later, and Luke was giving it large: 'These lads, they're good friends of mine, I can vouch for them; they're stand-up fellas,' he said to the Russian. 'I know them, they're very secure, honest and trustworthy. They would never grass you up. They're just interested in helping you with your business.'

At first, the Russian was stand-offish, and didn't seem interested. 'Speak to Luke,' he said. 'But not here, not tonight. Just talk to Luke, and I will get in touch with you.' He looked at me. 'I will come to your house tomorrow and we'll talk. It is safer that way.'

Decision made, I said, 'I'm one hundred per cent up for it. I'm ready to go for it.' I reached out and shook his big, powerful hand, and so did Paul.

I know what you're thinking: 'What a pair of mugs.' But the way we saw it, our lives were so shit, there was no hope or future for us in Leicester, and we'd never get another offer like that in our lives.

This deal did seem too good to be true and, of course, looking back with the benefit of hindsight, it was. But we'd known Luke for a long time and we trusted him. We wanted a short cut, a head-start in life to get going on it. So there was no turning back.

The very next morning, Luke and the Russian came to my house as arranged, to talk us through the finer points of the deal.

We were nervous as hell, and had already started drinking. We used to like a drink back in those days, and the impending meeting with Luke and the Russian had given us a proper thirst.

I'd talked it through with Paul. Luke had offered us both what we wanted on a plate, and we were both still keen to proceed. We told ourselves we'd only do it once, that we were being handed an opportunity we'd never get again. We knew it was dodgy, but compared to what life was offering us, it seemed like a risk worth taking.

When they finally turned up, we got straight into the nuts and bolts of the deal.

'Here's how it works,' the Russian said. 'When you get to Venezuela, you'll be fitted with bullet-proof vests that will contain five kilos of cocaine each. You'll get paid £5,000 each. Everybody in Venezuela will be paid off, so it will be a walk in the park.'

But I wasn't happy with that. I've always driven a hard bargain, and the drink gave me confidence. Five grand didn't seem like a lot for the risk we'd be running, so I spoke up: 'We're looking at a life stretch if we get nicked,' I said. 'So we want you to up the money.'

The Russian fell silent for what seemed an eternity, but then nodded. 'OK, we can make it £9,000 each. But no turning back. Double-cross me, and I will kill you.'

Fucking hell, this guy was hardcore, the real deal. He sounded merciless. But nine grand? We wouldn't get it until we got home, only the spending money, but that was a serious amount of cash to us: it could be life changing. That was tempting enough, but then Luke delivered the killer blow: 'On top of that, we will cover all of your expenses once you're out there,' he said. 'You'll get £1,500 each to blow. All your holiday will be paid for. Flights, hotels, everything. We'll even sort out all the tickets.' He smiled, all relaxed. 'Spend it on what you want – live a bit, get a tan. That kind of dosh will go a long way out there, lads. Hire a yacht, drink champagne, shag some prozzies, do whatever you want. You'll live like kings!'

That was it. *Ker-ching*, get in! We felt like we'd won the Lottery. *It could be you*? It fucking was! We were both totally sold on the idea now. The idea of prison didn't ever seriously enter our minds; we were totally sure it was all pre-arranged and sorted. And so, despite all the risks, and the threats to our lives, we were overcome by a tidal wave of greed. We put any worries to the backs of our minds and said yes.

Luke told us the Russian was keen to get us out there as quickly as possible. But we didn't even have passports.

This didn't seem to be a problem for the Russian. 'I want to move fast on this,' he said. 'Can you go today? But remember, once you're in, there can be no turning back.'

Before we knew it, events were moving so fast, we couldn't stop them. Part of me felt like he was trying to steamroller us into it as quickly as possible so there'd be no time for us to change our minds or bottle it. But even if we knew he was manipulating us, we were blinded by the money.

Paul and I hastily packed our bags, there and then. We lied to our mums and said that we were going on a booze cruise to France to buy fags and beer to sell at a profit, and we were off. We'd only be gone for a week. Or so we thought.

The Russian drove us to the UK Passport Office in Peterborough in a dodgy-looking old Sierra. It wasn't the sort of motor you'd expect a loaded drug dealer to have, but then we figured he probably drove this banger to blend in, lie low and not be too flash. He was clever.

After a lengthy wait, we got our passports, and the Russian bought us each a Ralph Lauren shirt to wear over the bullet-proof vests. We got them nice and baggy, as instructed, so they'd cover up the stash.

That same afternoon, we drove straight to London. The Russian took us to a dodgy-looking, dingy travel agent in Hammersmith and booked our tickets. They didn't even check our passports and he paid in cash, so there was no paper trail. It definitely felt like this was a place he'd used before, where they asked no questions and he told no lies. Then he booked us into a cheap hotel, and left us to it for the night.

The Russian told us we weren't allowed to go out, so we raided the mini bar and got absolutely hammered. We were so nervous about the following day, it was all we could do to try to relax. When the Russian came to our room the next day, he found us passed out, fully clothed and surrounded by empty miniatures, and went absolutely mad. He dragged us out of bed and into the car without even letting us get some breakfast. It was a grey, rainy day and I'll remember that drive to Heathrow forever: we couldn't wait to get out of the stinking country.

In the car, he handed us a wad of dosh each, all in US dollars. This was our £1,500 spending money. It was magical: we just kept smelling the sweet waft of those bank notes. We'd never seen that much money in our lives. Never mind cocaine – we were high on life.

As we pulled up to Departures, the Russian turned to us and said, 'You will be watched all the time by my people. Do not even think of cheating me or backing out. Remember what I said. I do not fuck about. Now, go.' And that was that.

It really was as fast as that.

We started spending the Russian's money straight away, on aftershave, 800 fags and a bottle of Scotch.

After boarding, and as the plane took off, I looked out of the window. The clouds were as one, a pure bank of whiteness stretching away into the distance, the sun rising over the top of it. It was the most magical sight I'd ever seen. We felt on top of the world. We had our trays down, which were covered in lagers and shots of whisky, and we were singing along to Oasis on our headphones. We screamed the words to *Slide Away* at the top of our voices, as we jetted towards paradise.

People were giving us funny looks, like we were two English thugs on the rampage, but we didn't care. Neither of us had been happier in all our lives.

CHAPTER 2

FROM HEAVEN TO HELL

We had no idea what Venezuela would be like, but in our minds it was all palm trees, beaches and girls in bikinis.

· When we touched down in Caracas, the first thing that hit us was the heat. We'd never felt anything like it. It was like a wall of hot air had crashed into us and we could hardly breathe. It was like stepping into a hothouse.

We were both still drunk from all the booze we'd polished off on the eleven-hour trip, and buzzing on life. We waltzed through Immigration, no questions asked, and all was going to plan.

Outside, we saw real palm trees for the first time. Not plastic ones, but real ones growing out of the ground. That blew us away. The roads were frantic with strange cars, and the air smelled so foreign and different compared to back home. All the way to the hotel, we were laughing our heads off. This was the life!

The hotel was impressive. For starters it was called El Paradiso – The Paradise. It had grand, marble steps leading up to its entrance, giant marble pillars, a polished marble floor and enormous rooms with balconies that overlooked a brilliantly lit swimming pool. Everything was plush – these guys had obviously spent money on us, just as Luke and the Russian had said they would. It seemed they were as good as their word.

We were party animals from the word go.

For the week we were there, we'd wake up and start boozing, bomb into the pool, then hang out on the beach. We decided just to get right on it and put the smuggling job out of our minds.

Being white as sheets and me with red hair and over six foot, we stuck out like sore thumbs, and girls would flock over to us wherever we were. With all of our money, they were like flies round shit. But what did we care? It wasn't even our money, so we spent it like there was no tomorrow. We'd order the girls food, and massive plates of crab and exotic fish would show up, with another crate of beers.

On the first night, we brought a couple of birds we'd met in a bar back to the hotel. The girl on reception went ballistic. 'No! You cannot bring girls like that in here!'

We thought she was just being a killjoy. Instead, I went to the room and knotted a few sheets together, tied them to a pillar and dangled them down from our second-floor balcony. There was no way we were letting that sour-faced old bag get in the way of the holiday of a lifetime!

The girls climbed up and we had sex with them all night long. But when they came to leave in the morning, they demanded money from us. So that's why the receptionist had gone mental – the girls were prostitutes! But we paid up – we'd had an absolute blast, and it really was a dream holiday.

It was paradise, but there were also little reminders that we weren't there just to party. One time when we were getting loud in a restaurant, a guy walked past us, went, 'Shhh!' and threw us a dirty look.

I said to Paul, 'Did you just see that?'

Paul nodded. 'Well, the Russian did say we were being watched.'

I had also noticed the same two blokes on a motorbike riding past a bar we were in, over and over again, staring us out.

At this, a terrible sense of paranoia kicked in, as we really felt like we were being spied on. We realised that this cocaine must mean a lot to them if they were watching us the whole time. And we also realised that we had spent so much of their money already, we were in debt to them. Now we owed them, and they owned us.

*

We'd been told to expect a phone call from our contact in Caracas, and on the second day, it came. A jeep would pick us up from outside the hotel at 8 p.m. the following evening.

The next day, it pulled up, on time. We put on our bravest gangster-like walks as we strode towards it, but really, my legs felt so wobbly with terror, I was amazed I didn't keel over.

We clambered into the jeep. It was really shitty, with wooden benches in the back and in bad need of a spray job. We'd expected a flash-looking car, but figured this was all part of the scam, to blend in and not draw attention, just like the Russian's old Sierra.

There were three blokes in there, and they were shady-looking characters. It was dark, of course, and with their dark complexions we could barely see them. But we could see they were carrying guns: we'd never set eyes on a gun in our lives. Their pistols were poking out of their jeans' waistbands – it was obvious they wanted us to see them; to send us a message and put the frighteners on us. We didn't have a clue what was going on.

I looked into Paul's eyes, and I could see he was scared. Sweat was pouring down my face, and I was chewing my lips with fear. But knowing he was there with me gave me strength.

No English was spoken, so it was completely disorientating. What were they talking about? Were they planning to rob us? Or kill us? What had we got ourselves into? Neither of us really knew. Our front rooms seemed a long way away at that point, and I'd never wanted to be there more in my life.

As he lifted his arms to be measured with a tape, Paul said to me, 'They must be measuring us up for the bullet-proof vests.' Suddenly, that made it real, and I got scared. We were having the holiday of a lifetime, but we were also here to do a job, and that day was getting nearer by the minute.

Suddenly, my heart started banging like a drum, so loud I thought they'd be able to hear it. I just kept looking at their guns and thinking, 'They could pop us off now and nobody in the world would even know we were here.'

They dropped us off back at El Paradiso and we walked to our room in stunned silence. Paul turned to me and said, 'Fucking hell, kid, we're in this up to our necks. There's no turning back now.'

* * *

What could we do but just get back to the partying? If anything, we went even more mental, to try and block out what was coming. We still had another three days of our stay left, so we decided to make the most of it.

The next morning, after a monster session at a night-club, we woke up with a Jamaican Rasta bloke asleep under our bed. We could hear him snoring and just see his feet sticking out. It turned out his name was Jimmy – we'd met him the night before and invited him back to our room, although none of us could really remember. Anyway, he asked us if we fancied some coke, so we gave him £10 and he disappeared off to score some.

It was kind of odd that we'd never really set eyes on any coke before, seeing as though we were about to smuggle ten kilos of the stuff, but it was the truth. We knew it was white powder, and that you took it up your nose, but that was it.

Three hours later, Jimmy was back with a lump of something, and started saying, 'Right, let's wash it up!'

We didn't have a clue what he was on about, but it turned out he meant to cook it up into crack.

All we'd ever heard about crack was: 'One hit and you're an addict.' To us, it was a serious drug linked with violence and squalor. But Jimmy brushed our fears to one side. 'So long as you don't inject it, you won't get addicted,' he said. 'Chillax, man.'

Jimmy cooked the cocaine up with some baking soda in a jam jar on the apartment's stove. And that was our first introduction to crack cocaine. Little did I know that we'd learned a skill we'd use many, many times over the coming years.

We didn't have any idea how much coke there was before it was cooked, but it was a big lump. It only cost Jimmy £1 a gram, and we'd given him a tenner, so you could safely say there were about ten grams there.

We'd been smoking it in the room for about three hours, enjoying the absolute buzz it gave us. I felt like I was flying, when Paul suddenly started going funny, holding his chest. He was sweating like a pig, his eyes were wild and he looked scared as shit.

'My heart, my heart! I'm going! Fucking hell, Jim, I'm dying!' he gasped. In that moment, I saw true fear in him. He'd obviously taken too much, and could have overdosed.

Jimmy started panicking, saying, 'Shit, man, you gotta take him to the hospital, now!' but Paul couldn't walk, so I had to carry him downstairs and bundle him into a taxi, shouting, 'Hospital, hospital, now!'

All the way there, I tried to calm Paul, saying, 'You'll be fine, kid, you just took too much,' but underneath I was panicking myself.

We raced to the hospital and manhandled Paul into A&E. There, the nurse took one look at him and frowned. 'Has he taken anything?'

Of course, I lied: 'No, no, he's just had a few beers.'

She flashed me a withering look; it was obvious by the state of Paul's eyes, his sweaty face and his panicked attitude what he'd been up to. A fool could have seen that, never mind a trained professional.

She gave him an injection to calm him down, which worked pretty quickly. After an hour we were free to go, but the thought stayed with me: this was our first-ever experience of cocaine and it had almost killed one of us.

What was the coke we were going to carry going to do to the people it was supplied to? If a few tokes could do that to Paul, what was ten kilos capable of?

We calmed down a bit after that – in fact, it felt like the moment when the holiday came to an end.

We had started to get a very uneasy feeling about the whole operation. What was going off? We knew these people had been watching us from day one, but as the last day approached and we got nearer to our journey home, our fear escalated.

Then, suddenly, we got a phone call telling us the arrangement was off.

Paul called the Russian direct, saying, 'Look, we've got no money left; you can't just leave us here to rot. Are you telling me that we need to wait here another three days, that the package isn't ready?'

It was torture. We just wanted to get on with it and get home.

* * *

After another three agonising days of waiting, neither of us slept much the night before we were due to leave Caracas and fly back to England. Apparently, the arrangement was on again, but the last-minute change of plan had left us feeling even more doubtful about it all. We lay there, tossing and turning all night, sweating and panicking about the task ahead. That was the first time I'd thought about what would happen if we got nicked, but I kept telling myself not to worry, as Luke had assured us that all the Customs staff had been paid off.

Then, finally, the day that we'd been dreading arrived.

We'd been contacted again and told to expect a jeep to pick us up outside reception at 11 a.m. The same clapped-out motor showed up, and we got into the back and started heading out of Caracas.

Away from the tourist area near the hotel, you could see that this was a poor country. There were kids dressed in rags and scrawny dogs everywhere. All the cars looked ancient.

We drove about thirty minutes out of the town, up into the mountains, and eventually pulled up outside a block of dingy-looking concrete flats. We went up to a flat on the third floor of a block, and straight away we knew we weren't hanging around with wealthy people any more.

I'd been expecting a glamorous pop star's apartment, or a Mafia mansion – something out of *Scarface*. But this wasn't even *Coronation Street*. In fact, it was more like *City of God*, that movie set in the slums of Rio de Janeiro. All the apartment contained was an ancient black and white telly and a battered old cooker, while the smell of the place was vile – this was definitely not like a drug dealer's house from the movies.

They offered us something to eat, but all they were eating were these sloppy black beans with rice, with a fried egg on the top. How could they eat that shit? Anyway, by now I was so nervous that there was no way I could have kept anything down – I'd have puked it all back up. We couldn't wait to get the hell out of there, to get the business done and just get on with it. We were both fed up of all the damned waiting.

The men fixed us a couple of drinks instead – we both needed some Dutch courage – and gave us a spliff to help us relax. 'You're good men,' they kept saying. 'You're good men.'

Trying to calm down, I looked out of the window. We could have been a million miles away from the four-star hotel, from the cocktails, palm trees and the beach. All I could see on the hillside outside were the shanty towns of Caracas, the shacks all made out of sheets of corrugated iron. It looked like a really big, ramshackle vegetable allotment. It looked exactly like what it was: a third-world country, full of stinking pollution, overcrowding, despair, poverty and danger.

One of the men vanished off behind a bead curtain. Soon they were all rummaging around out back, and we couldn't quite see what was going on. Naturally we started to fear the worst. What if they came back out and slit our throats? We knew they'd all have guns. With nobody knowing we were there, it was the most dangerous position we could have put ourselves in – and they knew that. The power was all with them, and they were playing good mind games. By the time they came back out, we were prepared to do anything they wanted.

Sure enough, a greasy-haired bloke with a gun suddenly came for us, screaming, 'Put your hands up! Put your hands up!' I only had time to think, 'Shit, what's going off here?' – I thought they were going to finish us off right there. But then they started laughing and instead pulled out a tape measure and started measuring our chests just like before. It was surreal.

They fitted us with green bullet-proof vests, the sort you see in American cop dramas on the telly. Only these vests weren't going to make us safe: all the padding had been taken out and replaced with blocks of cocaine. If anything, these vests were a death trap, a walking life sentence.

They fitted them to Paul and me, and I could feel the blocks of drugs digging into my ribs, hard, like steel fists. They were really, really heavy: there was a lot of cocaine in there. They'd told us it was five kilos each, but it felt much heavier than that. I tried to weigh up in my head how heavy a bag of sugar was, and did I have more than five bags there?

The weight and discomfort of the jacket combined to make it suddenly totally real. It was like something out of a video game. I kept thinking, 'Is this shit really happening to me?' But there was no way I was going to complain to these people. They were armed, they were dangerous, and we were now inside their circle.

I realised – with total clarity – that it was too late for second thoughts.

I soon snapped back to the real world as they tightened the vests as hard as they could, with a sharp yank that knocked the breath out of me. But the vests still hung funnily. It was pretty obvious we weren't just a pair of fat bastards, that we had something big and fat under our shirts; something that shouldn't be there – and which would surely alert even the most stupid copper or Customs official.

At that point, the guys started getting into a bit of a flap about something, which just heightened our panic. They were high on drugs, going off in Spanish, waving their shooters about and shoving each other around. It was mad as hell, all a bit trippy, and then a bloke came at us with a big sewing needle and shouted, 'Now we stitch jackets on!' and started to sew the vests onto us. Soon they were as tight as possible and didn't hang down so badly. 'This way, cops no notice! And you cannot take them off!'

They were making out that they were doing this so that we would look as natural as possible, but I wondered if it was so we couldn't change our minds and dump them if we lost our nerve. Basically, they were so tight, it felt like we were wearing straitjackets. We'd have to be cut out of them with a knife.

When you're that nervous, your heart's going like the clappers anyway; even without the vests we'd have been breathing oddly. But with the vests on, it felt like the life was being choked out of us – a sharp reminder that our breath, our very lives, could be taken away from us at any minute.

The guy who had sewn us up made us pace up and down the room, to make sure we could walk all right, and he gave us the thumbs-up. I was just thinking, 'This is heavy. We're never going to be able to get away with this.'

I turned to Paul and said, 'You look massive,' and he replied, 'You look a bit big yourself, like.' We even managed a laugh at that.

Then we put our shirts and jackets on over the top, so we were wearing the actual outfit we'd be going through Customs in. I looked at myself in the mirror and thought, 'Fair enough, we don't look that bad.' It looked like we'd been working out a bit, pumping the iron.

Our confidence rose at that point, but then we realised something: we were boiling hot. For starters, that was going to be a big problem in the stifling heat of Caracas but, more than that, we'd stand out badly, togged up in jackets like we were going out for a pint back home. But then, we reasoned, we were going back to England, a much chillier country, so the thought quickly slipped out of our minds.

'You're gonna take this stuff back for me,' said the greasy-haired bloke. 'And don't even think about making a wrong move, or trying to take the vests off. If you do, you'll be shot. We will be watching you at all times. Our people everywhere – in Venezuela, at the airport, back in England – they all have photographs of you. Your life won't be worth living.'

I looked at Paul, and I knew that he felt exactly the same as me: 'What the heck have we got ourselves into?' But we owed them. If we double-crossed them, they would probably kill us. There was no way we could get out of this now.

On wobbly legs, we got into a taxi for the airport. In the confined space of the car, it was immediately obvious that the vests stank to high heaven of chemicals – of cocaine. We didn't really know what cocaine smelled like, but a wild panic set in: if we could smell it, what chance did we have of getting past any sniffer dogs?

'Maybe this is a chemical they've sprayed on the vest to mask the real smell?' I said. Although we knew we were deluding ourselves, we convinced ourselves they must have wrapped the drugs in something strong-smelling to throw any dogs off the scent. I started bricking it.

Just then, The Fugees' *Killing Me Softly* started playing on the radio. For some reason it gave me hope, and I began thinking, 'We're going back to England, we can do this.'

But when we got to the airport, I was shitting it again. I told Paul I wanted to dump the vests in the toilets, but he said to me straight, 'That would be a death sentence, Jim. If we get back to England without the Russian's drugs, we'll be dead within a week. Forget about it, kid. It's too late to turn back.' Grim as it was, I knew Paul was right.

We walked towards check-in, and thought the whole world must know what we were up to: we were panicking so much, it was impossible to act cool.

Safely through that queue, we headed towards passport control, and suddenly my heart froze. 'Paul! Look, there's a sniffer dog by the gate!' Time seemed to stand still and my legs almost gave way.

Paul squeezed my arm. 'You're all right, kid,' he said. 'Keep walking and don't make it so obvious.'

As we handed our passports to the official, we had to stand right next to the dog. I swear it looked up right into my eyes. I thought we were done for, but it just looked away and we were told, 'OK, you can go through.'

Yes! Bloody hell, we didn't get nicked! Maybe it was true what the Russian had said, that all the guards had been paid to turn a blind eye to us?

I felt on top of the world at that moment. I thought we'd made it.

We got to the departure lounge and sat down, Paul just falling asleep on my shoulder the minute he parked his arse. All the stress and sleepless nights had finally caught up with him.

That's when I noticed two blokes staring at us, and muttering to each other. They were well dressed, in civilian clothes. Maybe they were undercover coppers? My heart froze and a surge of adrenalin made my eyes almost pop out of my head.

I shook Paul awake. 'Look, over there!' I rasped. 'Those two blokes keep staring at us! I'm telling you, this is the end of the road!'

Paul looked at them. 'You're just getting paranoid, kid,' was his calm response. 'Will you please just chill the fuck out?'

But I knew they were staring right at us. Once again, I suggested dumping the vests in the toilets. Again, Paul told me that would be a death sentence. It was an impossible situation.

Finally, our flight was announced. We walked down the tunnel to the plane and it seemed like it went on forever. Things were happening in slow motion. I could hear my heart beating in my ears. Sweat was rolling down my back, sitting clammy and horrible against the infernal vests we were stuck in.

As we rounded a corner in the tunnel, I suddenly clocked the two men who'd been staring at us in the lounge. They were standing in the corridor, just outside the jet's cabin door, which was tantalisingly wide open. They were searching everybody, frisking them under their jackets.

All we could do was carry on walking up to them, trying to act as naturally as we could. I felt as though this was happening to someone else; that it wasn't me. It felt almost like an out-of-body experience.

At the last moment, the guys looked straight at us, and stepped in front of us. These two men were the last thing between us and our flight home. We were so close to making it onto the flight, we could have jumped past them and into the plane. And then one of them said the words that will stay with me until I die: 'Put your hands in the air.'

Helpless, I obeyed, and the other man patted me down. Straight away he felt the hard resistance of the vest that contained my five kilos of cocaine. He paused, stared me in the eye and then smiled. The other frisked Paul and nodded to his mate. 'You two need to come with us into a room,' he said.

Our world came to an end and crashed down around our ears.

* * *

We were taken to a small, stuffy room in the airport that was packed full of angry, overexcited coppers.

'Now we do interrogation,' one of them barked, as he played tensely with his gun holster.

We were scared out of our wits. We had no clue what was going to happen next. We were just two ordinary lads from Leicester. We'd never been abroad in our lives. And now we'd been busted for smuggling ten kilos of cocaine and were being interrogated by armed police in a South American country, in a language we didn't understand. Nobody knew where we were. *We* didn't really know where we were.

Nothing can prepare you for deep shit like that.

There were what seemed like hundreds of people in the room: the two undercover cops who'd nabbed us; members of the National Guard who were dressed in army outfits with gun holsters, red berets and shit-kicking boots; and others who told us they were from Interpol. They were ready to nail us.

We were totally screwed.

Everything was happening so fast, it was impossible to take it all in. All the talking was done in Spanish – there were ten of them banging on at any one time, nobody spoke English and they didn't provide an interpreter. My Spanish began and ended at '*Cerveza* [beer], *por favor*,' so we might as well have been on Mars for all we understood.

As I sat there, trying to take it all in, I couldn't stop thinking about our arrest. A dodgy-looking guy had boarded the plane right after we'd been stopped and searched, and he'd looked back at us, flashing us a glance that had seemed to say: 'Don't you dare grass me up.' At that moment, it just seemed so obvious to me that the whole thing was a set-up – we'd been thrown to the lions so that he could slip around us unnoticed. It was a thought that would haunt me throughout our time in Venezuela.

I was convinced that he was carrying drugs, too. I felt like we'd been the bait, and he was the main man. Had the Russian done a deal to make the cops look good nicking us, but also thereby ensuring his drugs still got through with the 'real' smuggler? What were ten kilos of charlie to a cartel? Naff all. It was expendable – and so were we.

One of the armed guards smirked. 'This is thirty years in prison, boys, thirty years.'

I couldn't believe it. All I could think to say was, 'Oh, fuck.'

And he smashed me in the chest with his pump-action shotgun.

'You no say "fuck"!' he shouted at me. 'I see *Die Hard*. I know what "fuck" means.' A tiny, tiny part of me – the only bit that wasn't terrified – actually wanted to laugh at that. It seemed surreal that there we were, about to get Christ knows what punishment, and here was this twat talking about Bruce Willis. But I'd already worked out that laughing in the cop's face would mean another smack with his shotgun, so I shut it.

They cut the vests off of our backs with bowie knives and dumped them on a table in the middle of the room. The vests made a huge, heavy, clumping noise when they landed. There was a serious amount of class-A drugs right there, and I hated the sight of it, absolutely hated it.

Another cop sliced open one of the fat packages of drugs with his knife and put some of the contents on his tongue to test it, just like you see them do in the movies. He abruptly left the room and I thought, 'What's up with him?' It turned out that the stuff was so strong, it had instantly numbed his entire mouth and he couldn't speak. Obviously, we had been carrying some seriously powerful gear.

They sat me and Paul in opposite corners of the room with our backs facing so we couldn't see each other, and bizarrely started showing us photos of girls, shouting, 'Which of these prostitutes have you been with? We've seen you with these bitches!'

It occurred to me right then that the police had been watching our every move – we had seen some of these women at the El Paradiso hotel. We'd thought the hotel was our safe house. We later learned that we'd been staying right in the middle of a National Guard compound.

All our paranoia checked out – we'd definitely been watched all along: we hadn't been imagining it after all. It was just that we were being watched by the other side, too.

I desperately tried to piece things together in my mind. Had the Russian grassed us up from the very outset? Or had somebody in the hotel itself thrown us to the dogs? Had one of the blokes who'd fitted us with the vests grassed us up for cash?

Then my heart really started racing. I recalled the first boozy night out we'd had at the hotel, when we'd had a few too many drinks with a really cool French guy called Jacques.

It's fair to say we got wasted with him. As we shot pool and necked beers, he told us he was a diamond smuggler, and that that was where the really big money was. 'We're talking fortunes for that, my friends – £50,000 cash, each, for every run,' he said. 'It's a piece of cake. If you want, I can hook you up with my contact.'

This diamond-running game had sounded better than what we were up to – the cash was loads better. That night, Jacques had won our confidence, and so we'd confided in him about our drug-smuggling run. He'd seemed totally trustworthy, and as he'd told us about his scam first, we'd figured he was safe as houses.

Now my mind whirred: had Jacques been a plant? Had he told us a crock of shit about diamond smuggling to coax our story out of us? Or maybe he'd been busted and thrown our names to the cops to save his own sorry arse?

I was shaken from my panicked thoughts when a cop whacked me in the back with his gun, shoved me to my feet, then handcuffed me.

He frog-marched me and Paul out of the room and into a taxi that was waiting outside the airport. Even that was bizarre. Paul felt it, too, as he said, 'A taxi? What are we doing in a fucking taxi?' You'd have thought we'd be in a police car, or even an armoured van, but this was a regular taxi like the ones we'd been taking to nightclubs. Maybe we weren't so shafted after all?

But such thoughts were soon banished when the guard in the front pulled out his gun and said, 'You try and run, I shoot you in the head.'

I thought, 'Shit, this is serious now.' And then I thought, 'I'm eighteen and I won't get out until I'm forty-eight.' It was November 14th, 1996. We'd be old men by the time we got out in 2026.

If we lived to tell the tale.

* * *

The taxi wound its way up into the mountains for ages, until we reached a National Guard compound. Once in the checking-in office inside, they immediately took all our belongings – our passports, bags and jewellery: 'Right, rings off, earrings out!'

The ten kilos of cocaine were placed into a little cupboard, and then they marched us through several iron gates, finally ramming us into a stinking concrete room that, at about ten foot by six foot, was only about as big as a garden shed. There were no windows, it was boiling hot and it stank of sweat, fear, piss and shit.

Not only that, but we were crammed in with a few crazy bastards: one kept singing mad songs in Spanish, while another nutter was reading pages out of the Bible at the top of his voice.

We sat in that furnace, chained to the cell's bars like animals, for a terrible week. In all that time, we had no shower, couldn't shave and had to shit and piss in a bucket on the floor in front of everyone. We looked and stank like tramps.

Daytime wasn't so bad – at least we could keep an eye on the worst of the weirdos. Night-time, though, was a whole different ballgame. Trying to sleep next to who knew what sort of criminals, inches from a piss-pot stinking in the heat, our minds went into overdrive. I don't think I slept for more than an hour straight the whole time we were in there.

Food was plain rice with a boiled fish head in it. When I first saw it, I refused to eat it. We'd feed it to the army of cockroaches that swarmed all over the place. To be honest, the cockroaches looked more appetising.

Every time a policeman looked into the cell, we'd both demand phone calls home, or ask for a lawyer from the British Embassy to come and see us. But the cops would just wave it off and say, '*No comprendez.*'

Once we had calmed down a bit, we realised that we had to get our stories straight to have any chance of getting off. At the moment, we realised, they had us bang to rights. We decided to tell a couple of little white lies to try and lessen the blow.

'We'll stick to most of our story, but make out that when they sewed the vests on us, they held guns to our heads,' said Paul. 'We'll say we told them we'd got cold feet and wanted to pull out, but they threatened to kill us if we bottled it.'

It was only bending the truth slightly. Those gangsters in the flat did have guns, and both they and the Russian had threatened to kill us if we double-crossed them. So we agreed that would be our story. Paul had nailed it. He was always clever like that.

It took me two days to cry it all out. When the enormity of our situation hit me, I totally broke down: I was shaking, inconsolable, and cried so hard, I could hardly breathe. So Paul started singing Oasis songs to cheer me up. They were all my favourite songs and when he started on *Champagne Supernova* my tears of despair suddenly turned to tears of a profound happiness and hope.

Paul started softly singing the first magical lines on his own, but soon we were both standing and, at the top of our lungs, singing together. We were even standing like Liam Gallagher, with our hands behind our backs. We sang our hearts out, through the prison bars that separated us from the dark corridor where the perplexed guards would stand.

We were both crying our eyes out. Paul was my rock and this gave me something to cling on to. It dragged me from my pit of despair. We were scared, but we would not be broken.

After seven days in that squalor, a guard came in one afternoon and started making slitting gestures across his throat, saying, 'Today, you die ...'

We had no clue what was going on. Were they taking us to trial already? We'd had no visit from a lawyer, nobody from the British Embassy had been to see us, nothing, and nor had we been allowed any phone calls to our family. Nobody on Earth knew where the hell we were.

Suddenly, the door to the room flew open, and they dragged us outside, into the blinding sunlight. We hadn't seen daylight in a week; it was so bright, it physically hurt our eyes.

We were hustled across a yard and then up two flights of stairs and into an interview room. We were sat at a desk with a woman called Jackie, who was from the British Embassy. She quickly told Paul and me that they'd only just found out about us and our passports had gone missing. She tried to reassure us, but it was impossible to feel calm – in front of us were loads of TV cameras and a CNN news crew. They were throwing a bloody press conference!

At the front of the room was a table with all the packets of drugs on it, piled up, with some still in the bullet-proof vests. We stood there ashamed: our families hadn't even been told what had happened to us, so this would be the first they knew. I just wanted to die of shame for what I'd done to my mum and dad. We later found out that Paul's mum, Wendy, found out when she heard a news report on BBC Radio Leicester, which had picked up on the story. Only then did she find out where her son was. Having to live with that gutted him for a long time.

We were then interviewed on camera. We stuck to our story about being threatened with a gun. Paul was crying his eyes out, saying, 'They had a gun to our heads! We thought we were going to die!' It wasn't hard to be emotional, as we were scared shitless by what was going on. Not only by what was happening to us, but we also kept thinking that if this wasn't a stitch-up, then the Russian and his colleagues would kill our parents as we hadn't got the drugs back to him, and there was sod all we could do to stop it.

We were desperate and scared for our lives, but our sob story was naive: we were soon to learn that compassion in Venezuelan jails was rarer than rocking-horse shit.

After the press conference, Interpol questioned us, and tried to get out of us who our connection was. They promised us we'd be out in six months if we'd just direct them to our Mr Big, but we'd made up our minds that there was no way we were going to grass up the Russian. We knew we were involved in a cartel, and there are no excuses in that kind of business.

Obviously this wasn't due to any macho honour bullshit, like you see on the TV. The Russian had been perfectly clear that he would murder us if we double-crossed him.

We said to the guy it was no deal. This was it: one minute we'd been living the high life, and now we felt like our lives were over.

* * *

Back in the holding cell, we were finally allowed out to take a shower, so we reckoned we were about to be transferred.

There was a thief locked up in our cell who told us he'd been in and out of some of the worst jails in all of Venezuela for most of his life. As neither Paul nor I had any idea of even how to behave in a jail, we asked him what to expect.

'First of all, everybody in this country robs, from the baby to the president,' he said. 'And don't breeze past people – don't touch their asses, even by accident, as you walk past: you will get stabbed or shot.' He continued, 'You must get a knife on day one. That will be your guardian. If not, you will get robbed, raped and beaten. With no knife, you are going to hell.'

Knives? In jails? We thought the guards kept all that shit out. But the thief just laughed. 'My friends, you *gringos* have a lot to learn. You need to wake up – and fast.'

I tried to tell myself that he was just exaggerating to scare us. But he sounded pretty convincing as he told us how cons made knives out of metal taken from manhole covers or even the bars of their cells: by taking two razor blades and gluing them to lollipop sticks, they could gradually saw through the metal bars. You'd think it wasn't possible and it took them ages, but prisoners have a lot of spare time. Then they sharpened the metal to a fierce point on a wall or on the rest of the manhole cover. These homemade knives were the currency of any given prison, and much preferred to kitchen knives which, according to our source, were flimsy and snapped if they hit an opponent's bones. As knife fighting was mortal combat, he told us we needed a knife that could last the trials of battle.

We just couldn't believe what we were hearing. He was putting the fear of God into us, big style. But it got worse.

'The inmates have shotguns, pistols, and there are drugs galore, but if you have money you'll be OK. In our country, you can have as much money as you want in jail.' He laughed at our looks of surprise. 'There are millionaires in prison! Why? Because the guards want money in there, so they can take a cut of it. Corruption is everywhere. The guards are not there to protect you. They are there to take from you. Every day is a battle for survival. It's a jungle, and the weak will die.'

The thief, whose name we never got, told us there were two types of guards in the jails. The National Guards, who were armed with guns, could shoot you for no reason, and were renowned as sadists who should not be bribed. 'You cannot squeeze a fart out of a National Guard,' said the thief. 'They are tight, horrible bastards and will torture and abuse you.' He went on: 'The main staff are called vigilantes, and anybody can volunteer to become one so long as they didn't have a criminal record before they got in there. Those men, they can be your friends. Why? Because they are only paid $30 a month, and many volunteer to top up their pittance of a salary with bribes.' He grinned. 'After all, no man is going to risk his life with killers all week without some extra cash on the side. The government gives them a shotgun and a baseball cap, and shoves them in a jail and tells them to look after some inmates. That's it. They don't get any training. Get to know them,' said the thief. 'Offer them a drink. You can even smoke crack with the right ones.'

So you bribed the vigilantes to get all the guns, drugs and weapons into the jail, then the National Guard came in and took it all away while giving you a good kicking for good measure? It was absolutely mental! What kind of a country was this? What kind of a country allowed guns, drugs and knives in their jails?

On the eighth day of our time in the holding cell, they came for us at 2 p.m. Still nobody had told us anything about our sentence, or if there was going to be a trial – nothing. Paul and I joked shakily that they were treating us like mushrooms – keeping us in the dark and feeding us shit. All we had to go on was just that one guard at the airport, who'd told us we'd get thirty years. We had to assume that that was true, and that we were in this for the long haul. We just couldn't take it in.

We'd been given our stuff back as we'd entered the jail and the guard who came for us smelled of my after-shave: he'd been through my stuff and stolen it. My jewellery was missing, too. We were marched outside, through several iron gates, then shoved into the back of a jeep and handcuffed to a bar. Sitting on the long back seat, we had an armed guard on either side of us.

The guards must have been fishing that day, as the back of the jeep was full of stinking, gutted fish. It made us almost long for our shithole of a cell, which had smelled pleasant compared to this.

After another long drive, we came to a shanty town and pulled up at a five-storey police jail and holding station called La Vega, situated on the outskirts of Caracas. It was a huge, grim concrete block, with row after row of barred windows on every floor. At the time, we didn't know what this place was, or how long we'd be here. Even though we'd asked repeatedly, we just didn't have a fucking clue what was going on. And nobody understood a word we said.

At the desk where we were signed in, the police guard gave us our stuff back. Straight away, I knew we had a problem. In a British jail, you're in uniform and everybody looks equal. But here, we were just English lads, dressed in £90 Ralph Lauren shirts and Nike trainers. We were still in our holiday gear, the stuff we were wearing to nightclubs to try and pull birds. And now we had to walk into a jail wearing these togs. It was the first time in my life I wanted crap clobber, so I could blend in.

I took one look at my Nike trainers and polo shirt and knew they would make us a target for robbers the second we walked in there.

I said: 'Are you joking? I don't want it, mate. We'll get our fucking throats cut.'

He looked at me with cold eyes. 'No. You must take it. And now, you die.'

From upstairs, we could hear an almighty noise of men shouting, scuffling and rattling metal – knives? – against bars. It must have been the usual way to 'greet' a new inmate because all the cons kept shouting, 'Hey, *gringo! Gringo!*' Latin music was blasting out. It sounded like the last place on Earth you'd ever want to go.

We braced ourselves. I turned to Paul and said, 'That sounds a bit vicious.'

It turned out to be the understatement of the century.

CHAPTER 3
VIVA LA VEGA

As we were led up stairs to the first level of cells, it suddenly went totally silent. Men were hanging out of their cells between the bars, knives in their hands, clambering to get a look at us. I thought, 'Shit, this is it. This is hell.'

The armed guard opened the final iron gate to La Vega, and we were let in to a cell. We walked forward. We'd been over this moment many times in our minds, but nothing could have prepared us for the real thing. It was like our worst nightmare.

The heavy gate slammed shut behind us, the key turned and my arse was in my mouth with fear. The way this lot were eyeing us up, it was like they were cavemen and we were dinner. Everyone was looking us up and down, checking us out, like they were measuring us up for a coffin.

Suddenly, about eight of them surrounded us. They looked like local lads, all in their early twenties. They all had knives, which they were casually passing from hand to hand. They were like dogs or hyenas, hunting in a pack. They were obviously a gang – and they were about to try and turn us over.

I'd been mugged before, back home. I came from a rough and ready part of Leicester and knew how to handle myself in a scrap. Of course, it was nothing like this, with knives and gangs, but at that moment, my protective instinct – some deep-buried survival mechanism – kicked in. It was time: I knew we had to make a stand and front them out. This was our home now, for the next thirty years, and our lives wouldn't have been worth living if we let somebody come up to us and bully us like that.

'What do you want?' I said, pumped full of adrenalin, but secretly shitting it. I'm six foot and a big lad, whereas these lads were all around five foot five and scrawny, but they were armed. The ringleader – who had a tight, greasy afro, a nasty scar from his mouth to his ear and three fingers missing off his right hand – said in broken English: 'We want your clothes. And your trainers. Now!'

'Well, you can't just take them,' I said. 'We want food and cigarettes. Let's do a deal.'

It worked out. I didn't want my designer gear any more – I knew I'd get trouble every single day for it. So we gave them our jackets, they gave us some food and they backed off. I'd earned my spurs and we'd survived our first encounter.

But there were to be many, many more.

We spent that first night in a holding cell that was thirty feet by thirty feet, crammed in with about seventy other inmates. There were no mattresses, so we lay on the bare concrete floor, our heads next to the toilet, which was no more than a hole in the ground that was splattered with excrement.

Later, rats and swarms of cockroaches appeared from the hole and scurried over us. Prisoners argued, shot drugs, boozed, gambled and fought all night long. Sleep was an impossibility. Welcome to the Hotel La Vega.

We quickly learned that every day was pretty much like the day before. Name check was at 8 a.m., where we'd sit on the floor and the police would tap our heads with a wooden stick. Breakfast was at 9 a.m., but as there was no food provided by the jail, you'd have to buy ingredients from the shop and cook cornflour pancakes on a stove in our cells. The water was only turned on for an hour a day, but that wasn't guaranteed, so sometimes you'd be lucky enough to get a shower. Then the rest of the day was filled with working out, playing cards, listening to the radio – anything to make the day go quicker – until another roll call took place at 8 p.m. and lights went out at 9 p.m. It was relentless.

We'd been in La Vega for three or four days when we were finally allowed to speak with our parents. Jackie from the Embassy had been in touch with them and given them the number for La Vega. We were both in pieces and just kept saying, 'I'm so sorry. Sorry. Sorry.' They told us they loved us and they'd do all they could to help. I spoke with my mum, dad and girlfriend. They all told me to keep my chin up, but I could hear the terror in their quavering voices.

The worst thing was that our families had first found out about what had happened after the press conference at the airport. It had made big news back home, and apparently local newspapers had been calling them and going round their houses and hounding them for stories. We were putting them through hell, too. We knew the shame of it would be unbearable for them. Over four thousand miles away in Venezuela, it was a heavy cross to bear. We knew we'd broken our mums' hearts, and that killed us both.

In many ways it was the worst thing about it. We had given our all to get away from Leicester, but now we'd have given our lives just to be back home with our mums, having a Sunday roast or a cup of tea and feeling a comforting pat on the head. Feeling like lost little boys, we were relieved when we were moved a few days later into our own cell, and settled into a routine. We had to – to sit and think and try and fight the system would have been lethal.

We had also learned that, even though we were in jail, there were all sorts of businesses being run – and all with police backing. In one cell, a group of highly organised inmates sold coffee and cakes. Their leader was Pelon, a funny, bald man with a squeaky little voice who'd shout 'Happy!' in the morning when he brought coffee round. There was Robinson, a really tall fella whose grey, fuzzy afro made him look like Don King – if Don King had been a smelly, rotten crack addict. And then there was Diaz, who was a crack dealer, and weighed down with gold chains like Mr T from *The A-Team*. He was covered in horrible lumps that looked like boils, which we later learned were bullets that were still lodged in him. They were slowly killing him through lead poisoning, but he couldn't afford to have them removed. It turned out you had to pay good money to get bullets taken out in Venezuela. Just like the thief had told us in the holding cell, everything had a price, even life-saving surgery.

These lads bought their ingredients off the cops. It was the equivalent of twenty-five pence for a small bag of espresso coffee, and they'd sell it for twice that. They cooked on an electric element powered by two electric cables that ran from a sub-station opposite, and they had to pay the police £5 a week for the power. The electricity would, however, go off all the time and, of course, they had to pay the cops to have it reconnected. Both the cables were live, and they'd been connected to a metal element ripped off an old electric hob. With the cables attached straight to it, it would glow red-hot, and the boys would boil water on it and cook their cakes, which they made from a simple mix of flour and water with sugar sprinkled on top, on a skillet. To get the cables off the element, you had to whack one with a stick. You couldn't touch it, or you'd get your balls electrocuted off.

The boys who ran the coffee and cakes set-up had an open market: the cell opposite was a drunk tank where men were held for a maximum of three days before being sent to trial or transferred to another nick. They came in with all their money, straight off the streets, and as long as the coppers got their cut, we, as the inmates, were allowed to sell anything we wanted to them.

I soon realised that the crew who'd tried to mug us on our first day ran the whole show inside La Vega. They were a gang of bank robbers, and the leader – the brains behind the operation – was a vicious bastard called Bebe. He was the bloke who'd lost three fingers (in a bungled armed robbery, where he claimed the gun blew up in his hands) and you could tell he'd been in battles. Then there was Caha, Eddie and Alex.

This gang made most of their dough from the poor sods who ended up in the three-day holding cell. The drunks arrested straight from the street were thrown into the holding cell in their clothes, of course, with all their money, and other goodies, like watches. Bebe's gang, who were all tooled up with knives, would simply rob them of all their gear. If they resisted, they'd get stabbed in the leg or arm. Bebe's boys then sold all the stuff they'd stolen off the drunks to Diaz, who'd sell the watches to other inmates or to the cops. And with their money, Bebe's gang would buy crack off him. With all the extra money, Diaz then bought yet more cocaine off the police, which he turned into crack, and the cycle repeated itself.

The irony wasn't lost on me and Paul. We couldn't believe it. We were doing thirty years for cocaine offences, yet here we were, in a jail, where the cocaine was being supplied by the very same police who'd locked us up for smuggling it! What was more, those corrupt cops were turning a blind eye as Diaz ran a drugs empire right under their noses. Right there, we knew the whole Venezuelan prison system was fucked beyond belief. It was totally lawless, and rotten to the core.

At that point, I absolutely detested hard drugs. They'd got me into that mess, and I hated myself for that. As far as my life went, drugs were public enemy number one. My anti-drug fury rose even more when, a week after we'd arrived at La Vega, we were taken to court for our first official hearing.

Handcuffed, we were treated like maximum security prisoners – four guards smashed us in our backs with machine guns and piled us into a van. We felt as though we were being treated like serial killers or suicide bombers. I know that drug smuggling is wrong, but we were treated so appallingly we both felt sub-human. At the courthouse, we met a National Guard sergeant called

Ramos for the first time: a big, nasty fucker who bossed people around and never once smiled. His uniform was pristine, covered in badges and, worst of all, he looked exactly like Saddam Hussein.

In 'court' – which was a tiny room with a desk and table – was the judge, a woman in a miniskirt who was caked in make-up and dripping with jewellery. We reckoned that she looked more like a prostitute than a lawyer, but probably got paid a whole lot more. The whole episode was a complete farce. Our interpreter didn't show up, and everything was being said in Spanish, so we hadn't got a clue what was going on. We were simply told our farcical 'hearing' was over, and we were to go for a medical on the way back to La Vega.

On the way back, something so unbelievable happened that it completely confirmed to us that we had been set up all along. Not only that, but it was a total shock to see just how far bent the coppers really were.

On the way back from court, the police van we were travelling in suddenly slowed to a halt, parking up right outside El Paradiso, the hotel we'd been put up at by the Russian and his gang. In stunned silence, we looked on as the guards filed out and bought cold beers from our old hotel bar, then brought them back to the van. They opened their bottles and blew their beer breath through the grille. It was torture. Then something truly gob-smacking happened: the guards racked up lines of cocaine on the dashboard and started snorting them.

Barely able to comprehend it, I said to Paul, 'I bet that's the stuff they took off us. Effing hypocrites! They locked us up for drugs and here they are doing it in front of us!' It made us furious. Here we were outside the very hotel we'd been staying at, locked up in a van and being treated like the worst kind of rapists, while the cops did coke and drank beer.

It was 100 degrees outside, and they kept us there like that for four hours. You wouldn't do that to a dog. When they took us in for our medical, they wanted a urine test, but we were so dehydrated, we couldn't wee.

After that experience, things fell into place for me: I said to Paul, 'We're gonna get forgotten about here – we're fucked. We won't get any sympathy from anyone. We're never going to get home.'

* * *

Shortly after we arrived at La Vega, we'd learned via a British Embassy official that a local lawyer was prepared to get us out if we could raise £20,000 in cash. Of course, we didn't have money like that. I had no savings, and my parents lived in a council house, so there was no way they could sell it. Paul's folks owned their house, but he would have had to get his family to remortgage it for that kind of money. There was no way he was going to do that after putting them through this much trouble and shame, and I couldn't blame him. We fronted up to the fact that we'd be there until we got the whole nightmare sorted out for ourselves.

Around the same time, I had my first prison visit from my dad. It was incredibly emotional, and I felt so ashamed of what I'd done. We found out that our story was all over the papers and telly back home, and that our local MP, Keith Vaz, had been speaking about our plight in the House of Commons, and even paid for Dad to fly out to see me. I knew I'd always be eternally grateful for that.

Keith had also told my dad the full horror of Venezuela's notoriously bad human rights record, which was well known to international protest group Amnesty International. Amnesty told him 360 prisoners had died in custody in the last four years, while torture to obtain confessions, appalling overcrowding and insanitary conditions were the norm. In 1994, 100 prisoners had died during a riot and fire in Sabaneta jail, and thirty had been burned to death in La Planta.

He also said that there was no extradition treaty between the UK and Venezuela, so there was no hope we could be sent back to the UK to serve our time there. As you can imagine, this totally screwed me up. This just couldn't be happening. The fear was so intense, it was a sour, electric, bitter taste in my mouth, as though my fillings were on fire.

But my dad told me to keep my chin up, and just focus on staying alive. He told me the family back home needed me to stay strong, as they were going off their nuts with worry, as any parents would.

He also told me he'd been busy looking for the Russian since everything had gone wrong. My dad used to run the doors of the clubs in Leicester and knew what was what. But the Russian had simply disappeared. He'd vanished into thin air and nobody had a clue where to find him.

I think we were just looking for answers. We still didn't know if he'd grassed us up or not, and not being able to find out was agonising.

While Dad was in Venezuela, he'd decided to go on a tour of some of the jails in the country with British Embassy officials, to try and get the inside line on some of the places we might end up in. He visited the notorious La Planta jail and when he told me about it, to my horror it was his turn to start crying. He just couldn't help himself, so I knew it was deep emotion, something that had never come easily to old-fashioned, macho blokes like him or me.

'I don't want you going anywhere near that place, son,' he'd said. 'I've seen them walking round with grenades, guns and machetes; just walking round willy-nilly with them. It looks terrifying.'

When Dad left to go home, it was tough. It had been amazing to see him and had given me the strength to face another day – something I really needed – but we were fast approaching our first Christmas inside, a time both Paul and I were dreading.

* * *

Our first Christmas posed a major test of moral fibre. Christmas is always a lonely time to be away from your family, let alone banged up, abroad, as you feel so far from home. Then, it really hammers home.

To help us through that first fateful festive season, Paul drew a huge Christmas tree in wax crayons on the wall of our cell. It brought out our soppy side and gave us a positive focus, instead of constantly worrying about getting killed. Paul always was wicked at drawing, and that tree helped lift our spirits when we were at our lowest ebb.

We put the Christmas day date under the tree, and had carol services and drinks in our cell. Being a Catholic country, Christmas in Venezuela is a big deal. On Christmas day itself, we all shared local food: cornflour mixed with meat and olives, which is the Venezuelan version of roast turkey. We could hear the revelries on the streets outside while even the biggest cons exchanged small gifts. It wasn't the same as back home, obviously, but even in that hellhole, Christmas was seen as a time for giving and reflection.

Somewhat bizarrely, and probably due to the fact that we were foreigners, we received an invite down to the prison governor's quarters for his Christmas day party. This was seriously weird shit. We thought the guards hated us, yet now they wanted to invite us over for festive drinks and nibbles?

We didn't want to go for two very good reasons. First, we told each other, the governor's quarters were down on the fourth floor, which was where all the female cons were banged up. We'd seen the women on our way into the jail – they were rough as badgers' arses. Second, and more serious, we knew that all the Venezuelan prisoners in La Vega would think we were grassing them up for their drug deals. They'd surely think we'd get pissed and sing like canaries about who ran what and what was stashed where. Even though that's the last thing we'd do – we knew that would be certain death – there would be no telling vicious bastards like Diaz that when we got back.

Such was our prison paranoia – a depressing thing to live with, but something that we realised would help keep us alive – this seemed like a set-up. I told the cops we didn't want to go, but a quick slap to the face made it clear our attendance was compulsory.

Making a big show of reluctance, we dressed in our best clothes – plain white T-shirts and cheap blue jeans – and headed downstairs to the governor's quarters. Half an hour later, there we were with the governor, Martinez – a seriously scary, big guy with a Marines moustache – eating sausages, when we suddenly clocked a couple of decent birds who were doing the cooking. It was totally surreal to see them there, but with the free booze and grub, we filled our boots and started to chat to them a bit.

I met a lass that night called Siyanni, who was inside for drug offences. She used to be a model and drugs were a big part of that world. She went on to be my girlfriend, while Paul got chatting to a girl called Kiki.

Through the bars of the windows we could hear salsa music blasting out in Caracas. It was kicking off out there, yet it was agonisingly beyond our reach.

A few drinks in, and we heard loads of banging coming from outside and looked out the barred window at what we thought must have been fireworks. But when we looked closer, there were no fireworks, just a young lad standing on a rooftop of one of the shanty houses, shooting a machine gun down at five cops, who were returning fire. The 'rat-a-tat' of the gun sounded like firecrackers, while the bullets were lighting up just like fireworks, and tearing through the night sky. Only it was a full-scale gunfight going on between the cops and a kid. The guards saw us looking and ushered us away from the window.

We could tell the party was winding down, and at that moment I sobered up. In my mind, I was thinking about what was going to happen to us when we got back upstairs. I knew Bebe and his gang would pull knives out and interrogate us, so in desperation I stole a fork to defend myself, which I slipped up my sleeve.

Shortly after, we were taken back upstairs and, as predicted, everybody was waiting for us, looking fit to explode. As we walked back in, I muttered to Paul, 'We're gonna get it here.'

Bebe, Caha, Eddie and Alex cornered us, and Bebe snarled, 'You grassed,' and pulled a knife. I had thought through what I would do in this situation, and was ready for him. Again, it had to come down to not seeming weak – if they saw how scared we were, we'd be sitting targets for their mindless violence.

I grabbed his arm and put my fork to his throat. Now we were in a situation. 'Fuck you!' I said, right into his face. 'We've said nothing! We're like you!' Then I played my ace card: 'If we grassed, the cops will turn the place upside down in the morning. If they do, kill us then.' It was a risky strategy: I was worried there might be a random search the next morning, but thank God there wasn't.

We'd proved we could be trusted and, for a while, things simmered down.

The inmates of La Vega were a strange lot. There were killers, bank robbers, kidnappers and bombers everywhere, but we realised quite soon on that they were all really immature. As a consequence, it was easy to sidetrack them to help defuse situations.

Paul was a master at this. For example, Bebe would go ape about something petty like his coffee going missing, and we'd start singing UB40, Oasis or Beatles songs.

It would confuse them into submission. They'd go, 'What the hell is that?', and the next thing you'd know, we were giving them a lesson in English music. We'd tell them that the Brits were the kings of rock and roll. They'd argue that salsa was better. It didn't really matter – but they'd forgotten that a minute ago they were ready to whip out their blades or shooters. Paul really was brilliant at that kind of diplomacy. It showed that there was another way than the law of the fist, and it became a very clever tool.

Paul would also cleverly take the heat off us by plucking on the other cons' heart strings. While they had visitors, like their mums and dads, it was obviously rare for us because of the sheer distance and expense. So we'd make an issue of that, and the cons would start to feel sorry for us. It was like a game of chess: confuse the enemy, and make sure you end up on top, and alive.

When we first got to La Vega, I was amazed by how many of the inmates believed in nonsense like voodoo and fantastic, mythical stories. It wasn't long until I saw a voodoo ritual being performed, and it scared the shit out of me. A man had drawn a pentagram on the floor and placed a red candle at each of the five corners. During the possession, he'd made these awful, demonic growls – it was pure evil and very frightening. The man had thrashed about madly on the floor, saying in a totally different voice: 'I'm your Viking, and I am here to protect you.'

He had drunk from a bottle of rum like it was water, and smoked cigar after cigar. He also started slashing at his tongue with his razor. Blood had been oozing out of his mouth, yet the next day, when I saw him, he not only didn't remember a thing about the possession, but he did not have a single mark on his tongue. I am not bullshitting: it was the strangest thing I ever saw. Other inmates would sit there in white robes, frantically puffing on cigars, then letting the ash fall onto a piece of paper. Some so-called expert would then read the ash, a bit like Dot Cotton might read tea leaves.

It was total bollocks, but they believed in it. Perhaps they had to. The system didn't allow for anything else for them to trust in – the level of casual cruelty and lack of care inside was astounding.

Many times in La Vega, I witnessed men in terrible pain, only for the guards to totally ignore their pleas for a doctor, painkillers and even a much-needed trip to the hospital. Apparently, they had bigger fish to fry than ridding inmates of agonising pain – like playing cards or jacking off to confiscated porno mags.

One particularly gruesome time, I saw a guy sewing up his own arm after he'd been badly wounded in a machete fight. He'd been struck on the forearm, the blade had gone right down to the bone, which it had cracked, and a big flap of flesh was just hanging down. His veins were pissing out blood – he'd virtually had his arm hacked off. He kept soaking the blood up with a rag, and every time he pulled it off to inspect the damage, you could see right inside his arm. It was making me feel so ill, I had to walk off.

When I had gone into his cell half an hour later, there he was sewing the flesh back together with a regular needle we used to repair clothes with. He'd smiled at me: 'I've got it numb. I took a few tranquilizers.' But I knew his tendons had been severed, so I said, 'What about internally?' He'd just smiled with glazed, druggy eyes, and said, 'It all fits together.' Amazingly, he survived.

Another con made a good living as a dentist. His services were very much in demand, as guards didn't give a shit if any of us got toothache. He was an old boy, with little round specs and a black leather dentist's bag containing all the proper kit: he really looked the part and we all trusted him. This guy went round pulling rotten teeth, and had performed hundreds of extractions. He'd earned a reputation as a diamond geezer and was a real asset to the jail.

One night, he got stoned and admitted he'd never been a dentist in his life: 'I just thought I'd help people out and make enough money to get by,' he said. We called him The Invented Dentist after that. Despite no formal training to speak of, he was brilliant. He was a true artist, really clever. He even made me a perfect gold tooth to replace one he'd pulled out. It fitted like a glove and I was really annoyed when I lost it one night during a scuffle with a thief.

I also discovered the Venezuelans have a novel cure for trapped wind. I was sitting in our cell one day, doubled up with terrible indigestion, when Bebe said to me, 'Lie down on your side and keep perfectly still; I will get the gas out of you.'

He took a sheet of newspaper, and rolled it into a cone, stuck the thin end into my ear, and set fire to the big end. I heard it crackling for a bit, then 'Voof, voof!' – I swear, the cone sucked something out of me. Bebe said the cone and the heat had drawn the wind out of my ear.

'Are you trying to tell me I just farted out of my ear?' I asked, incredulous.

Bebe replied, shrugging, 'That's just the way we roll. We don't do doctors.' To this day, I don't know what happened, but my indigestion had completely gone.

Another time, Paul had a saucepan of boiling water knocked onto him by accident when he went to strain some spaghetti he'd cooked. When it went all down his stomach, almost getting his bollocks, we feared it had burned him badly, and he'd have an agonising blister to deal with.

But a guy nearby who had seen it happen said, 'Wait there!', and threw instant coffee powder on the wound, telling Paul not to brush it off for fifteen minutes. After Bebe had got me to fart out of my ear, I thought anything was possible, and made Paul keep the stuff on. After a quarter of an hour, all he had was this tiny, little red mark and no blister. The coffee had drawn all of the plasma from his skin, like some kind of miracle cure.

The inmates would also use aloe vera from a cactus for cuts, too. With no doctors on hand to help, and hospital visits by doctors either off bounds or too expensive, they just had to be self-taught experts in getting by. Luckily, as *gringos*, Paul and I did get slightly better treatment on occasion. One such time was marked by my dad sending me a pair of Bermuda shorts. I was glad to have some new shorts, if only for a rather bizarre, if funny, reason. When we'd been at the hotel El Paradiso, we'd hung around with those prostitutes and now, three months on, a weird lump had appeared on my John Thomas. I told Paul, and showed him my foreskin, saying, 'What's this here?'

He replied, 'Looks like you've got a genital wart there, kid!'

At the time, it didn't seem to add up. Surely it'd been too long ago to have been something I'd picked up in the outside world? I got talking about it to the other cons, and the bank robbers – Bebe and his mob – confessed that they'd been stealing my Calvin Klein underpants to wear for when their girls had come to visit them. They'd done this without me noticing, 'borrowing' them from where I left them after washing them, then hanging them back up where I'd left them to dry. They thought that wearing designer pants would impress their ladies, and I reckoned they'd passed on their gremlins to me.

Whichever way I'd got it, word got out, and the commissary came up and demanded I showed him my willy in front of all the other inmates. There were two transvestites in the holding cell at the time, and they got all excited, telling me they loved men with red hair.

The guards took me to hospital and put me on a drip. They stood there and watched, with their rifles drawn, as they waited for the contents of the drip's bag to drain into me. They never even touched my dick; I have no idea what was in the bag, but the lump cleared up overnight!

When the new shorts came in from my dad, I was relieved to say the least – close-fitting clothes like my Calvin Kleins were obviously not suited to the climate, or the culture of 'borrowing'. Even better, Dad had stashed thirty quid's worth of local currency in the inside pocket.

As he'd left after visiting me, Dad had given me quite a bit of advice: 'Don't let anyone know you've got any money, and if you need money, go to the toilets and only take out what you need. Never take out money in front of anybody.'

But I should have known that a Venezuelan thief will stop at nothing to get what he wants – the money led to my first serious confrontation, and was the beginning of my reputation as somebody who should not be messed with.

That night I pulled a sheet over me and went to sleep, wearing the shorts, with my money stashed inside as Dad had instructed. I vaguely remember having a dream about a man floating over me in the night and, in the morning, that dream turned into a nightmare when I realised that the money had gone.

I just flipped. That money was my dad's. I knew it would have been one of La Vega's many crack addicts who'd done it, so I walked straight into the main dealer Diaz's cell, grabbed his little oppo, Jordan, who did all the thieving, and hoisted him off the floor.

Rushing over, Diaz drew a knife and put it to my throat. 'Put him down, or we'll have you killed.'

'I'm not fucking having this!' I roared. 'I want my money. You've got an hour to get it.'

I'd got the balls about me now; I'd woken up to it all. But they told me the money had gone. They'd already given it to the cops to go out and buy cocaine. For all I knew, they'd probably already smoked it.

I never got my money back, but that £30 loss bought me something you cannot put a price on in jail: respect. A line had been drawn in the sand. They knew I'd be prepared to step up and fight things out if anybody ever stole off me again.

By this time, something had changed in me. I'd tried to play it straight in La Vega, but being a nice guy didn't get you anywhere. It just got you fucked over. I had to toughen up. In part, this was down to my frustration at the language barrier. I couldn't explain myself to them in Spanish, but they understood when somebody talked with their fists. On top of that, my mounting anger at being abandoned and left to rot without any form of a fair trial was giving me a shorter and shorter fuse. I took to the violent side much more easily than Paul, who was always much more diplomatic, more able to think. He had decided early on to learn Spanish, as we'd already had a couple of court appearances where we didn't have a clue what was going on. And as we mostly couldn't understand what the other inmates were saying, it further added to our sense of isolation and paranoia, something which made me edgy and ready to scrap.

At first I'd said to Paul, 'Sod learning Spanish. They can speak English!' but I knew that was just being daft. I'd never been much good at school, but knew we had to adapt to survive.

Paul started me off, teaching me the words for everyday objects, like pen, water, soap – the basics. Gradually, my vocabulary grew. Lots of the other inmates wanted to be taught English, so Paul would give them lessons in return for them helping us with Spanish. And because I could see they wanted to learn, it helped break down a barrier in me. Paul was absolutely right to talk me into those lessons. It's bad enough being in any jail, but being in one thousands of miles from home where you don't understand anything that's being said was just too disorientating.

* * *

After the stolen money incident, I got another chance to prove myself just weeks later when, about four months into our sentence, Jacques – the French diamond smuggler who we were still convinced had grassed us up to the police – walked up the stairs.

Talk about what goes around comes around.

I said to Paul, 'Hey up, it's Christmas!' When Jacques saw us, he just went white.

I'd become good friends with a pretty deranged guy called Loco – Spanish for 'crazy' – who had a big crazy beard and wore a sheet wrapped round his head that made him look like he was in the Taliban. He looked the part, all right.

When I explained to him how I thought Jacques had double-crossed us, Loco said to me, 'Jim, what do you want me to do to this man? You want me to rape him? To stab him? Kill him?'

I said, 'I don't want you to do anything to him. I just want to talk to him. I want to have it out with him. I just need to know if he grassed us up.'

Later that afternoon, me and Loco cornered Jacques in the toilets. He went into a panic, droning on that he had had nothing to do with our arrest, that we were all in this together.

I just said: 'Loco, warn him for me.'

At that, Loco dragged him into a cubicle, and went berserk, shouting, 'I will stab your fucking legs off if you grassed my friends up! Did you put them in prison? Did you?'

Jacques was shitting himself, screaming, 'No! It wasn't me! It wasn't me!'

Loco looked at me to see what I wanted to do. I could tell he was worked up, though. I calmed him down by saying, 'Don't stab him. Just take what he's got and leave it.' I pacified him by letting him take Jacques' money.

Jacques had to suffer a mugging and have that treatment, because we'd all had it. It was just a rite of passage at La Vega: you turn up, you get mugged. It was best I did it – it didn't get out of hand.

So Jacques had denied everything, but it still just didn't sit right. Nobody else had known anything about our scam in Venezuela. All day I sat brooding, convincing myself it was him and vowing to teach him a lesson, even though Paul wanted nothing to do with it. Of course, I had no proof Jacques had set us up, but paranoia and my general mental instability made it make sense at the time.

When the lights went out at 9 p.m., I told Bebe and all the boys the story. Bebe offered me a knife. But I said no: 'He's going to get it English style. I don't need any weapons.'

Working myself up into a proper red mist, I walked up to Jacques, grabbed him by the neck and lifted him off the floor, walking with him like to slam him into the wall; at which point he punched me hard in the chest. I dropped him hard on the floor and his head fell onto a metal rod that was sticking out of the concrete floor. He went right on to it, ending up with a big gash all the way down the side of his head. There was a big pool of blood, too. He started jerking and I thought he was dead, but then he got out a big nail clipper he'd got in his pocket that had a knife on it, and he went for me.

I bellowed, 'Come on, then!', but at that point all the lads jumped him, and the guards burst in and dragged him away to hospital – where he would need twenty stitches.

This was a serious situation. Ramos, the National Guardsman who looked like Saddam Hussein, came in and shouted: 'All of you! Against the fucking wall! Drop your trousers round your ankles now!'

Once all twenty inmates were facing the wall with their bare arses on display, the guards came in with their big, metre-long metal swords, and smashed them all across their arses with the flat of the blades. Even though they always hit like that, it didn't stop the swords cutting, and skin was hanging off their buttocks, with blood pouring down their arses. They were howling in agony.

Everybody got hit apart from me and Paul. For now, the guards were still afraid to hit us for fear of the British Embassy finding out. But they made us watch – and they knew many of the inmates would hold us personally responsible for what the guards did.

When the guards had left, Bebe – who, by now, was the leader of the whole prison – turned to his gang and said, 'Nobody is telling them that Jim did it. Jim is a good man. Paul is a good man. Anybody tells, I will kill them.'

The incident didn't end there. A day or so later, Pelon lost it in the yard, and threatened to tell the police it was me, but once again Bebe threatened to kill him, and he backed down. To Bebe, grassing was the ultimate sin a con could commit against a fellow con.

I never did make any sense of the Jacques incident. Was it him who'd grassed us up or not? Who knows? In my mounting anger and frustration, I'd lashed out. If I got the wrong man, I'm sorry. Looking back at times like that, where I turned to violence as a solution, I don't like what I did. But I was so full of anger, it took over my mind.

Paul could see a change in me, too. He'd often ask me to calm down. I could see a fear in his eyes at those moments, and I knew I'd gone too far. He'd say, 'You can't keep going around with weapons, and turn to fighting. There'll always be somebody madder than you, they'll just pull a gun and shoot you dead. We're in this together. I need you. Don't go getting killed on me.'

Like that, Paul would drag me back from the abyss, and I'd feel ashamed of my violent behaviour. Paul was my calming influence. I needed him as much as he needed me.

Shortly afterwards, Jackie visited us from the British Embassy and told us that our original thirty-year sentence had been reduced to five years – for drug possession not trafficking. Unbelievably, they'd tried us without us even being there. Keith Vaz, the MP, had been talking about us in the House of Commons again in a bid to show the world how outrageous our situation was.

It was all comforting news, but as there was no extradition treaty Jackie said it was unlikely we'd be back on British soil before we'd served our full sentence. We went back to our cell with mixed emotions. We wouldn't be old men by the time we got out now, but whether we made it out of this dump alive, who knew?

Not long afterwards, though, I discovered something new to help me survive. Bebe had been impressed that I'd stood up to Jacques without a weapon. And one day, he took me to one side and said, 'You English, you are not pussies. But you cannot fight like this any more with your hands. You need to become a Venezuelan. You need a knife. I will make you a special knife.'

He measured me from my wrist to the tips of my fingers, because a Venezuelan fighting knife has to be the length of your hand. Two days later, he came back with a length of sharpened prison bar and said to me: 'Anybody can shoot a man dead with a gun. But it takes a real man to use a knife. Here is your knife. This is your mother now. Your mother. Do you understand? Take it everywhere with you. Don't ever let anybody else touch it.'

It was round, weighed about two kilograms, and had been sharpened to a vicious point. It was more for impaling than cutting, and it was more than capable of killing. We had been accepted.

It can't be overstated just how important knives are in the Venezuelan street and prison culture. A Venezuelan's choice of combat is knife on knife. They don't do boxing or karate or anything like that. It's cold, hard, unforgiving steel. Knives are a part of their native street life: it's what they are brought up with. It's seen as an honourable way of giving a man a chance, rather than just killing them stone-dead with a bullet to the back of the head, which is looked upon as a cowardly way of killing or sorting out conflicts.

In Venezuelan jails, if you robbed somebody of their 'morals' – like stole their stuff, or disrespected them in any way – then you had to be prepared to fight that person with a knife. But there were strict codes that operate during knife fights, and if you failed to observe them, you could be shot dead on the spot by anybody watching. Make no mistake, it is a deadly serious business – with the emphasis on the word 'deadly'.

Come the age of seven, most South Americans have learned how to fight with knives. Like the bare-knuckle boxers in our own gypsy culture, it's an integral part of their culture. If you win, you're known on the circuit.

A knife fight worked like this: before a knife fight could start, you had to stand sideways on, with one foot touching your opponent's. These knives were not for slashing. Fighting with them was for mortal combat, to the death. These weren't penknives, but sharpened, two-kilogram lengths of prison bars.

The 'killing point' on a person is from the breast to the head. That's where all the best knife fighters would go for, and a sharpened prison bar or manhole cover could easily penetrate a man's chest and kill him stone-dead with one thrust.

Of course, some men survived. I saw a man stabbed through the face and it came out of his cheek on the other side. The winner almost got killed for that: it's bad form to go for the face; you're not allowed to do that. Men don't like to have to live with the shame of having a scarred face for all to see for the rest of their lives.

In La Vega, I used to see them practising knife fighting at night with sawn-off broom handles with rags tied round, which had been soaked in candle wax. The rags were lit, so you could just see the flames arcing around like something out of *Star Wars*. You'd hear them – 'Voof, voof!' – going through the air. It was mesmerising to watch.

The flames wouldn't kill, but they'd burn. When they connected, it went 'Tsssst' – you could hear the skin sizzle like a steak on a barbecue – and it hurt like hell. But it was better than death, and you never made the same mistake again: I got marks all over my torso and arms when I was being taught by Bebe, and other skilled knife fighters, later on in my time in Venezuelan prisons.

I got really into the art of knife fighting, because I knew it was about pure survival. You carried your knife with you everywhere, even in the showers, when you'd keep it between your teeth to show you weren't to be fucked about with.

The week Bebe gave me that knife, I saw my first serious knife fight. One day, three new guys came in, covered in scars, looking like they'd done a few knife fights. They took to us, but one morning I woke up and the knife Bebe had given me – which I slept with under my pillow – had gone. Even though our cell was locked, somebody had got in. It was unreal. By now, thanks to Bebe, nobody would have been mad enough to take my knife.

Bebe hit the fucking roof. He stormed outside, and a minute or so later, I heard him smash one of the guys' heads against a wall. He'd searched his cell and found my knife. He threw it at the guy, who was black, and said, 'You took it. Now, you have to earn it!', while pulling his own knife.

An excited rabble of men circled, and the duel was on.

The guy lunged for Bebe, but he was too quick, too agile. The black guy was tall, so Bebe could get him from any position. Being small in a knife fight is an advantage as there's less to aim for, less to hit.

The guy tried to get Bebe in the face, but Bebe went low, stayed under the guy's thrust and forced his own knife up and into the black guy's arm. It was over in seconds. He dropped to his knees, screaming, and the guards burst in and dragged him off to hospital, as he was leaking a serious amount of blood. Bebe could have killed him, easy, but he just wanted to show the prison that this guy was easy pickings. He just wanted to humiliate him.

Bebe gave me the knife back, and a serious bollocking. He shoved the knife into my hand and said, 'Now fuck off, I don't want to see that thing ever again.'

When Bebe took my jacket just minutes after our arrival at La Vega, he became my first enemy. He was the first man who had shown me any aggression, the first man who pulled a knife on me.

But, over the months, he became my mentor. He was getting us ready for what was to come, when we realised that we couldn't just sit back and serve our time. Bebe taught us that we had to fight if we wanted to survive. We had to wake up; this was our new way of life.

I had started to turn – and there was no going back.

* * *

By now, we'd been to court about fifteen times. There had never been an English interpreter available and nothing seemed to be moving forward at all, so we decided that it was time to take matters into our own hands and go down the route of attempting to buy our way out of this mess.

We contacted the lawyer who'd originally asked for £20,000 to set us free, and told him we wanted to do business. His name was Mendez.

My dad managed to scrape together £5,000 and get it to him, and in return he promised us he could get our sentence reduced from five years to four, but said we could get out in as little as seven months for good behaviour.

We were very excited by this, and had high hopes for our next appeal. However, it was left to Jackie to tell us that our sentence had actually been increased to ten years. There was no explanation: it was just what the judge had decided.

This lawyer had fed us a bunch of crap. We were incandescent with rage. We'd been totally stitched up.

CHAPTER 4

INSIDER DEALINGS

In time, we came to realise that the only way to get on, to get money, swim rather than sink, was through drugs. More than that, he who controlled the drug trade controlled the prison.

Because La Vega was only a police holding cell, there tended to be a very quick turnover of inmates. The vast majority of cons were only there for a few days, until they were sentenced and sent to a higher security jail. Other cons like Bebe and his crew were there for longer, awaiting the outcome of some drawn-out appeal, but even they tended only to be residents for a few months.

Paul and I were the exceptions to this rule. As we were British, it was decided that it would be too dangerous for us to be placed in a maximum-security jail. We were to stay at La Vega indefinitely.

Because of this, it wasn't long before we found ourselves among the longest-serving cons in the whole nick. Robinson had been set free and Pelon had been moved to La Planta, so we stepped up, took their cell and claimed their coffee and cake business. Then, when Bebe was released, myself and Paul found ourselves at the top of the tree.

We were running the operations at La Vega.

One day, a big African guy called Amen came into La Vega. He told us he'd still got eleven 'thumbs' – a thumb-sized roll of drugs – of heroin wrapped up in plastic in his stomach. Each thumb was eight grams, so he was holding 120 grams of pure heroin, which was a huge amount of smack, and worth a serious amount of money.

He'd tried to smuggle about thirty thumbs of heroin, but had been caught by Venezuelan Customs. Amen – nicknamed because he was a serious Bible-basher – told us how he'd eaten bowl after bowl of jelly to prepare his stomach for his deadly cargo. It's the best way to safeguard it – in a protective bubble inside your gut.

Although he'd been caught and the police had made him shit out the majority of his stash, somehow he'd still got eleven left inside him when they let him go. And so we did what any caring, sharing con would do, and immediately sent out for some laxatives to get the drugs out of him.

He went for a shit, and came back a little later with the drugs, which he'd thankfully washed clean.

'Listen, you'd better not double-cross me,' he warned. 'Don't you dare rip me off.'

I replied, 'You're lucky you've come into a jail like this where everything is controlled by us. If you'd have come in here last month, they'd have taken that off you and given you fuck all. They would have stabbed you and given you shit. But we're here now and we'll take care of you.'

At that moment, I realised we'd gone from jail novices to much more hardened cons. We'd had to toughen up, but that had meant we'd lost part of our real selves. It was sad. Our environment was turning us into people we didn't even know.

We began selling the heroin to addicts who came into the holding cell and were desperate for a fix. Pretty soon, we were earning a serious amount of money, more than we ever could selling coffee and cakes. Selling drugs really was the easiest and quickest way to make money in a Venezuelan jail. And money meant power, which meant *protection*.

Amen told us he had a friend, Patrick, another African guy, coming in soon, with eight more thumbs of heroin. He said, 'You've got to respect Patrick. In his country, he's a prince.'

I had laughed and replied, 'Hang on a minute, that's in Africa. You're in Venezuela, mate. Here, he ain't shit. Don't tell me how I need to treat people.' Paul and I had been in La Vega too long to start giving up our position at the top.

Patrick came in, and he started acting like a prince all right. He went and shat his heroin into a bucket, and brought it back covered in shit. He expected me to clean it for him. And he only gave me two thumbs.

'Hang on, where's the rest of it?' I asked.

And he replied, 'I'm not giving you all of it, you'll rip me off.'

I called Amen over: 'Amen, did we rip you off? No. If you want to hold it, fine, but if you get searched or mugged by a knife-wielding psychopath – which can be arranged – you'll lose the lot.' I explained to him that his best bet was to give us all of his drugs so we could safely hide it for him.

Our hidden goodies had never been found. As weapons cost a fortune, and guards would seize them at every opportunity, stashing knives and guns out of sight of the beady eye of the law had been elevated to an art form.

In La Vega, I'd got up to fifteen knives hidden in my room at any one point. The prison walls were rough and rustic, and the concrete mix was soft as shit, so you could easily scratch away at it and make hidey-holes for weapons. We'd moulded a brick out of polyester resin we'd had brought in, painted it to look exactly like a brick with modelling paint, and kept it in the wall. It looked just like a real brick, only it was hollow behind and we could slide it in and out.

As our final trick, we put it in the bottom row of bricks near the floor, because when the guards came round and knocked the walls to check for stash holes or escape tunnels, they always tapped the middle of the walls, but never the bottom – the lazy sods couldn't be bothered to bend down.

Finally, to really confuse the guards, we'd cover our walls with elaborate drawings of naked women, Bob Marley and the occasional Christmas tree – then we'd plaster posters everywhere, of Oasis, Ninja motorbikes and topless girls from *Loaded* and *FHM* magazines, which the Embassy brought in for us.

When a guard came in our room, he'd stare at our pictures and totally forget what he was looking for. We had it sussed.

I never saw eye to eye with Patrick. He was just too big for his boots, so I decided to teach him a lesson. He'd been walking around with all of the money he'd made on the heroin – which we'd sold for him – in this big, fat money belt. He was also too showy, too cocky – playing his music at maximum volume and making cell life difficult for everyone around him. I knew that sooner or later he'd get damaged for it.

I decided to beat the others to it and mugged him myself. He'd cried, 'You can't take from me, I'm a prince!', but I picked him up by his belt anyway and shook all of his money out.

I didn't know it at the time, but that mugging would later come back to haunt me.

*

Business was good. We were getting twenty-two grams of cocaine delivered every day by the police, for which we'd pay £20. They would deliver it directly to Paul, as bold as anything, then watch as we cooked the cocaine with baking soda – or with ammonia floor cleaner for an even more addictive high – on our stove, powered by electric cables that we paid the cops to wire from the sub-station. Everything we needed, we'd get the police to call in. Paul was the chef, and I'd watch the door.

We'd get a big biscuit of crack – we called them cookies – from five grams of coke and sell a stone, or rock, for the equivalent of 50p to the piss-heads next door in the holding cell. We were easily trebling our money, plus we could buy even more coke to cook it up – the cycle repeated itself.

We didn't want to get involved with selling heroin direct to users, as it was considered scuzzy. People looked down on the heroin addicts. They were the bottom of the food chain, as they'd pass out and soil themselves. They stank and would become crazed when they needed their next fix. And they were more likely to overdose and die, and if you'd supplied their drugs there could be severe payback. The further you could stay away from users, the better.

Instead we'd sell heroin to a corrupt cop called Flores for £40 for an eight-gram thumb. We'd hit it off with Flores straight away. He'd buy us a bottle of rum for £10 – they were only £5, so he doubled his money – and he'd smuggle it into us in an empty yoghurt carton, or once, inside a hollowed-out baguette, which was jauntily poking out of a grocery bag.

Paul and I weren't using coke or crack ourselves, although we enjoyed weed. When we were selling the coffee and cakes, we were just doing it to keep busy and kill time. We weren't really earning enough cash to buy treats like chocolate or rum.

But when we started selling drugs, we could suddenly afford computers, TVs and radios. I even bought a mobile phone. It was a big, poxy Motorola flip thing, but it did the job. Now, we could call our families back home. The police used to get us credit for the phone, so we were set up nicely. We were in a crazy moral dilemma: if we dealt drugs, we could get more of what we wanted, like hearing our mums' voice. We knew dealing was wrong, but things like that were a lifeline. It helped that we'd earned a reputation for ourselves to keep our new belongings safe

Flores brought the mobile in, but we had to be careful. He liked his money and could be bribed easily, but nobody else could find out as that would have been going too far. I paid £50 for that blower, which in there was the equivalent of £500 in the UK, and I couldn't even send texts on it.

One evening, as Paul was phoning his mum, gunfire broke out. When she asked what the noise was, he had to tell her it was the TV.

My dad suggested we got a camcorder to film what it was really like in there. Paul thought it would be a good idea: 'Nobody will ever believe us when we tell them there's guns, knives and drugs in here. Let's film it to prove it.'

I arranged it via my dad. The footage is well disturbing to watch, even now. There are clips of both of us with guns, acting like gangsters. That's not really us, but yet another example of how we had to adapt to stay alive. We became like that to fit in, to get by. We were off our heads most of the time. You had to be, just to get through the day. Weed just numbed it all, and made it go away.

When you're in a shit hole like that, believe me, reality is your enemy.

Running the drug trade also meant we had to dole out some harsh punishment. If you didn't, everybody would take the piss – and, believe me, there's no bigger piss-taker on earth than a crack addict in need of a fix.

One time, a crack addict stole off us, and we sat him on the cooking element to brand his arse. That was his badge of shame. Every time he went in the showers in every prison he ever went in from then on, he would be known as the lowest form of thief. It might sound brutal, but to deter a crack addict from theft, you have to resort to drastic measures. These animals would steal their grandmother's false teeth for their next stone of crack. They had to be taught a lesson and we had to keep reinforcing our position at the top of the tree just to survive. It was the way life worked in there.

It was around about this time, about eight months into our time in La Vega, that two landmark events happened: we started using hard drugs, and I bought my first gun.

When I'd first been chucked into La Vega, I'd been very anti-drugs, as I'd seen them as the reason we'd thrown our lives away and ended up in this shit. But by now, we'd been inside for getting on for a year and the crushing boredom just got to us. And working with the drugs every day had its own set of temptations, in so far as we saw first hand how the effects of them could take you out of that hellhole. Plus we knew we'd always have a constant supply as we didn't actually have to score drugs: the police delivered them directly to our cell. Drugs became an escape route, and you didn't even get punished for possession.

But we also saw first hand the dangers of doing the white stuff. While we made sure to only dabble with the hard stuff, some people were so hooked, they had destroyed themselves doing it.

The worst I ever saw was a mad-headed Spanish kid called David. He had a ponytail and would kiss his muscles and grab his cock, saying, 'Who wants a piece of the Big Daddy?' He'd been caught for cocaine possession, and was looking at a long stretch, and it just tipped him over the edge.

His dad would come and visit him, and he looked mega rich, like proper Mafiosi, with top clothes: a silk shirt and cravat, a hat, all very elegant. Every time he visited, he gave David a big chunk of money, and he came straight to us, begging for cocaine.

David was around for about two months, and I never once saw him eat, but this guy would inject about eight grams of cocaine every day. He'd mainlined so many times, most of the veins in his arms had exploded, so he'd inject the drugs into his neck, between his toes and even in his dick.

One time, he jacked up in the communal shower room just outside our cell door, and one of his veins exploded all over me, covering me in his blood. It was absolutely gross.

When David couldn't get cocaine, he'd go mental and smash himself against walls. One such time, he grabbed two live cables that were sticking out of our cell wall. When I asked him what the fuck he was doing, he smiled manically, saying, 'It wakes the cocaine up in the system!' It was unbelievable: I knew those cables packed a punch – when a guy from the BBC had come to interview us, he'd leaned back on them and the current had sent him flying across the room and set his jeans on fire. This journalist would come and see us as often as he could and was a great supporter of our plight, so we felt bad for him.

*

Paul and I had plentiful supplies of cocaine so we would always skim a bit off each stash we got in, making up the shortfall with laxative powder. I used to crumble crystals of crack into a spliff – we'd call it 'bread with cheese' – and just blaze it. Paul was always more into coke, but I'll admit I was soon doing crack every day. It was just what you did in jail. When I was released from jail, and exposed to the British price, I just thought, 'I'm not paying that for this shit!', and I never did drugs again. I'm totally clean now. But then, it shames me to admit it, I was a pretty major crack head.

But I did have some standards. I always drew the line at smoking crack from a tin can like a proper addict. I'd seen too many times how this kind of behaviour could rob a man of his soul. It was always disgusting how those addicts ended up: they were the lowest of the low.

As for the gun, by this point we were making just too much money not to have one. Of course, you ended up paying at least double the market value, but owning a gun became a matter of life and death for us as soon as we started churning out serious quantities of crack.

I wanted to make sure I got a good gun. I went for a Python .357 Magnum six-shooter. That cost me £300, which was paid for with our crack money. I only had it for a few months, and never fired it, but you had to have the ultimate deterrent if you started in the drug dealing game. We were just too high profile to be relying on knives any more. It was known that my attitude was: 'Fuck it, I'll just shoot you if you take my stuff.' And it worked. Luckily, that was a threat I never had to carry out. But the fear it might happen was the deterrent I needed.

The subject of conjugal rights – prisoners having sex with women while in nick – is a sensitive issue in Western jails. But in Venezuela, it was routine – so long as you had enough money and bribed the right cops.

In La Vega, for the equivalent of eight quid, the guards would take us downstairs and let us spend the night with our girlfriends in a cell reserved for such activities.

We only found out about this while getting drunk one night with the police downstairs – they were happy to do the drinking, so long as we did the paying.

The floor below us was where the female inmates were held. There were about twenty of them at any one time, and we had contact with them about twice a month, because every time the British Embassy came to visit, we would get to talk to them down there. As the only *gringos* in La Vega, especially big lads like us who dwarfed the locals, the girls were always curious about us. We always made sure we finished up with the Embassy officials five minutes early, to have precious time to talk to the girls. It really helped keep us sane.

We used to send messages down to girls we liked, and we always got letters and drawings back. One day, after a bout of steamy messages – my Spanish was much better by now – I decided to up the stakes a bit and sent a message to the girl, asking if she'd send up her pants. She flipped. In the past, she'd lived in Plymouth for three years, and said, 'I know the English, and you're a pervert!' I told her Plymouth was a pretty uptight place, not like real cities like Leicester or London, where anything goes. I think I got away with it.

She had a bully of a boyfriend called Nando – like the chicken restaurant. We had a run-in and because he was a judo expert, I had found myself reduced to throwing hot coffee in his face, badly scalding him. Oddly, she'd liked that. It wasn't your usual courtship, but then we weren't in a usual place.

For my nineteenth birthday, the guards charged me £20 for a room with a bed, and I got to spend the night with one of the girls I'd met. The female cons were watching through the bars, but I didn't give a shit: this was my first contact with a woman in over a year.

It could get political, though: a female copper called Munro caught me having sex one time. She had always flirted with me, but became a complete bitch after she saw me with someone else! Another disastrous time, I was having sex with a Puerto Rican girl in a broom cupboard, when I felt a cockroach crawl over my arse. I kicked the door open, and the floor was swarming with them. What a passion killer.

*

There were lots of horrible insects and other foul critters that used to make our lives miserable in La Vega. Cockroaches were everywhere, and you'd often see huge, hairy tarantulas crawling around. But they were all tame compared to *avispas* – big, black, evil-looking hornets. They were about two inches long, and were pitch black with horrible, long legs, black wings and bright orange feelers. They lived in grim cocoons that hung all over the jail and looked like they were made of mushed-up cardboard, like those bottles you have to piss in in hospital. They used to kill massive tarantulas with their powerful venom, then drag them back to their nests, where they ate them.

These things were vicious bastards, and would fly straight at you. And if you flicked one away and it hit a wall it would sound, 'Ching!', like it was made of plastic. Paul and I used to joke it was like they'd been sniffing cocaine. They had that attitude. They were the crack addicts of the insect kingdom, which seemed pretty appropriate considering where we were.

Not only were they aggressive; they seemed to have photographic memories, too. One day in La Vega, I realised an *avispa* nest had appeared outside the bars of my window. The constant buzzing and threat of a powerful sting was doing my head in so I decided to do something about it.

I waited for most of the *avispa*s to leave the nest one morning, then I bashed the cocoon loose. It fell down to the street, where it hopefully landed on a copper's skull.

I thought the returning *avispa*s would follow their nest down to the pavement, but one was a cheeky shit. Later that afternoon, I was having a kip after reading the Bible out of boredom, when I woke up looking like John Merrick, the Elephant Man. My face was swollen like I'd been battered with a mallet.

The locals took one look and said, 'Quick, quick!', and put two hot knives on a cooker. Before I knew what was coming, blam! – they put these two hot knives on my face. All this crap went 'Pssssht!' from the lump, and a load of dark red blood that had gone bad came out of my face.

It turned out this bastard *avispa* had stung me and snapped its sting off in my face. The locals told me the *avispa*s bury their sting in your flesh, then wiggle their arse until it snaps, whereupon it flies off and grows another sting before it even gets back to the nest! They pulled it out: it looked like a thorn or a splinter, and was an inch long.

One of the constant grinds about being in jail was that every time you rose to a beef and took action against somebody who'd robbed you or otherwise done you wrong, it led to a never-ending cycle of tit for tat.

People were always trying to wind us up, but we had to choose our battles, or we'd be fighting every minute of every day. And, in the end, you'll always find somebody harder or more unhinged who's willing to kill you without losing any sleep.

But, every now and then, it was impossible to turn a blind eye. That's what happened one day when some twat threatened to rape my mum.

About ten months into my stay at La Vega, my mum and dad came to visit me from Leicester. It was the first time Mum had been over, and I was excited but also nervous, because of the obvious heartbreak and anxiety I'd put her through.

Nothing was going to spoil this visit. My mum was the most important person in the world to me. So, I had bribed a guard to let us use a special, private room that you could use if you were rich enough. It had its own sink and toilet which, as La Vega went, was like staying in The Savoy.

We were having a good old natter, through hugs and tears, when one of the drunks from the tank shouted out, 'Hey, *gringo*! We're gonna rape your mum good! We'll rape your bitch!'

I told him to shush, but he kept going on. 'Fuck you, *gringo*. I will kill you!'

I looked at him and said, 'Yeah? We'll see.'

My mum told me not to worry about it, but I was seeing red. She didn't speak Spanish and didn't understand what he'd said. But I did. My mum had had to scrimp and save every penny to get out to see me and I wasn't going to have anyone insult her like that. I vowed to get my revenge on the twat that night.

Later, with Mum safely packed off, I crept up to the bars of his cell. There was an eighteen-inch gap between the bars to his cell and ours, and I reached out with a small mirror to see where he was.

I located him: he was lying down, kipping, his face was sideways on to me and he hadn't seen me creeping up on him. Silently, I moved down to where he was and loudly whispered, 'Hey up, geezer!' When he opened his eyes, I said, 'Hey, I'm the English man from earlier today. You said you were gonna fuck my mum?'

He started laughing, dead cocky, but he got more than he bargained for. I'd got a can of cockroach spray and a lighter and, at the exact moment he started to laugh, I shouted 'Fuck you!' and used the lighter to set fire to a blast from the can.

It was like a blowtorch: it went across him and flared his eyebrows, his hair and everything. He was screaming, shouting, 'You fucking English bastard! Screw you!', as he rolled around to beat out the flames. But he didn't say anything else after that.

Every incident like that had consequences. Everybody wanted to knock you off your perch – and you had to go back at them with attitude, or it would just keep happening.

Another time, I was idly chatting to a Swiss mate of mine when some bloke in the next cell threw a big bowl of piss over me.

I went mad, completely mental.

In revenge, I boiled up a massive aluminium food dish of water, and poured salt in it. I dragged it to the door, where they were asleep on the floor, picked up the pot and threw it all over them, scalding them. They were screaming their heads off, and the guards piled in as I shouted, 'That's what you get for chucking piss on us!'

The guards got me up against the wall, and I got smashed across the arse with the sword for the first time. The two lads I had chucked water on were covered in huge blisters.

Things were getting out of hand for me. As the cycle of violence continued, there had to be fallout, both physically and to the person I was becoming. Where would it all end?

I had lost count of the number of times we were taken to court during our stay at La Vega, and I'd totally disengaged from the process. The whole thing just depressed me: I knew we had no chance of freedom. Every time we went to court, it seemed like an opportunity for them to psychologically torture us.

We'd get there, and the judges would take the piss out of us. They kept laughing at us, saying things like, 'You will get put down for many years. Look at me, I'm with a nice woman, I own nice things, but you are fucked. I can see you looking at that car there; I have one of those, but you never will!'

The whole system was fucked up: it was completely corrupt and only about money. But even though we had money, we couldn't get out, so what was the point in even going to court? I felt we were a novelty to them: two English lads on a drugs rap. They'd hit the jackpot, and wanted to make an example of us; to throw the book at us and break our souls.

So, with another humiliating appearance due, I closed our cell, and over the course of six days solid, I smoked eight grams of heroin with Carlos, who was a proper addict. Paul could do nothing for me. I was so down, I just wanted oblivion.

The morning of our court date, they chucked us in the back of a truck, but I was so monged out that I had no idea. In court, I could see everybody looking at me, but I just wasn't interested. I shut off to it. Lo and behold, nothing happened that day.

Another time, about a year and a half into our sentence, my parents were over and arranged for an interpreter to be at our next court appearance. We were excited that at last we might be able to make our point and get some action.

When the guards turned up to take us to court, our transport was three motorbikes. They handcuffed us to the back of these bikes with us wearing nothing but shorts and flip flops, then wheelied through town, machine guns strapped to their backs. They scared the shit out of us so much, then rushed us in and out of court so fast, we couldn't even remember what happened in there.

*

For fourteen months, I'd been harbouring a serious grudge against Mendez, the corrupt lawyer who'd run off with £5,000 of my dad's money after we'd mistakenly tried to buy our way to a shorter sentence. He'd vanished with the five grand – and our sentence had been increased to ten years – leaving us seriously cheesed off.

They say revenge is a dish best served cold, but in my case, revenge was to be a dish served by a sly bastard called Jesus.

One day, I was reading the local newspaper, when I clocked a picture of this lawyer. He had on a massive Rolex watch.

Jesus, who I was pally with, happened to be a thief from a Venezuelan street mob called the Rolex Gang. He was inside La Vega for his part in a huge spate of notorious, murderous Rolex thefts, and he'd bragged to me before: 'I can tell if a Rolex is real or fake from over the other side of the road, *amigo*. Don't walk around my neighbourhood if you're wearing a Rolex, because you'll end up dead. We have special eyes.'

I knew Jesus wasn't bullshitting. He was the real deal. He had told me how, before he got to La Vega, he had stolen a guy's crack and smoked it all, passing out in an alleyway in a drug-induced coma. But the guy he'd robbed had found him, and had rammed a machete right through his chest as he slept. Jesus had been so out of it, he was only woken by the sound of the machete slamming into the concrete, after it had passed right through his body. The jerking motion had woken him up, not the pain.

The blade had narrowly missed his heart and, since then, Jesus believed he was blessed. I didn't exactly see it that way – another scar all the way under his armpit where a guy with a machete had tried to chop his arm clean off his body did little to convince me Jesus had led a charmed existence. He'd often show us this battle scar; in fact, he had so many scars, we nicknamed him Frankenstein. In short, Jesus was not the sort of bloke you'd ever want to double-cross.

So, just to test the water, I threw the newspaper over to Jesus and said, 'Jesus, I want you to sort that twat out for me. He's a lawyer called Mendez: he ripped my dad off for five grand and did one. He's left us in the shit. We can't find him.'

Jesus looked at the picture and said, 'I won't do it for you. But I will do it for what's on his wrist.'

I didn't think anything else of it. It was just one of those throwaway things we talked about, to pass the time of day.

Within two weeks, however, news of Mendez's death appeared in that very same newspaper. He'd been robbed and killed – for being flash.

I said to Paul. 'What have we done?'

Mendez had got what was coming to him and wouldn't rip anybody else off ever again. But had we inadvertently got him murdered? And if word ever got out that we'd played a part in Mendez's execution, would we rot here in Venezuela forever?

Because so many new cons were admitted all the time, many of them carrying valuable cargos, fresh ways to make money always presented themselves at La Vega.

One time, six *Yakuza* – Japanese gangsters – were thrown into the drunk tank wearing flash suits, expensive watches and with pockets full of US dollars. Some of the boys had ordered them to strip to their underpants, at knife point, and robbed them of everything they'd owned before they'd even smoked their first fag. I told them the *Yakuza* weren't usually the kind of gang you'd want to fuck with, but they didn't give a shit about that: they'd never heard of them.

Two years into my time there, two flash-looking young Spanish guys called Andres and Emilio were admitted, and they were carrying an expensive-looking leather briefcase. Straight away, Paul and I sniffed an opportunity, and ushered them into the protective environment of our cell.

They wasted no time in telling us they were serious cocaine dealers, who smuggled huge stashes of the powder into Ibiza in the hollowed-out doors of a Mercedes. They were proper European drug lords, and were telling me about all the Ibiza parties they'd go to, with wild, drug-fuelled orgies afterwards. They also took most of the charlie we got into La Vega: they were serious party animals. They paid us over the odds and everybody was happy.

A main source of getting cocaine into La Vega was via the drug mule Carlos. He'd been caught smuggling a huge batch of coke with his wife, Isabel, but he'd taken the whole rap so she could go free. After her release, Isabel had stayed in Caracas and was moving drugs for Carlos on the streets. She would then pass him the narcotics and the money she'd made dealing during visits to keep him flush.

When Emilio heard of this connection, he asked Carlos if Isabel could go and visit one of his cocaine contacts in Caracas and then sneak a 'serious amount' of the drug into the jail. Naturally, Emilio would pay well, so the deal was arranged.

During her next visit, Carlos's wife smuggled the drugs into La Vega, they got safely to Emilio, and we were all set for a major party. Two Arab lads supplied all the booze. They didn't touch the coke, but loved a drink, and reasoned Allah would forgive them if they prayed on a Friday.

We were all sitting playing cards when Emilio and Andres walked in with the drugs. I'd never seen anything like it. They had so much gear, they filled half a coconut shell and put it on the table in our cell, saying, 'Help yourselves, boys, tonight the party is on us.' That coconut was overflowing with powder.

Back then, I didn't touch coke, but even I had to admit that the coconut was a beautiful sight. Emilio told me there was something like 800 grams in there – the best part of a kilo.

I had decided to have a few sniffs when Carlos suddenly said, 'How do you guys like my wife's pussy?'

Confused, we replied, 'What are you on about, mate?' He told us that the drugs we were all sniffing had been smuggled into La Vega inside his wife's vagina, in tied-up condoms.

There was a stunned silence, then Emilio said, 'Love. It's a beautiful thing.'

We all laughed 'til we cried.

As the party continued, it was clear Emilio was over the moon. 'This shit will last me a month,' he said, but I knew that, now he'd exposed it, it wouldn't last long.

'What do you mean, exposed it?' he asked. I told him that the very best cocaine 'evaporates' in prison – I'd seen lines of cocaine racked up in La Vega, and the person had turned to their mate for a few seconds to talk, and when they went to sniff it, it would be gone. All that was left on the table was a greasy smudge. You had to be quick.

When Emilio heard this, he shrugged and said, 'Well, we'd better get it on then, boys!' We were dipping our thumbs into it like it was sherbet and sniffing it like lunatics, drinking rum like it was water and blasting out salsa. Coke was spilling over the edges of the table and onto the floor, but there was so much of the stuff, nobody was bothered.

We ended up locking ourselves in our cell for four days until we'd sniffed that coconut away: no sleep, day and night, T-shirts off, sweating, all the way through. Emilio and the boys didn't leave our cell until every last fleck had been consumed. Afterwards, I slept for three days straight.

Soon after, when we'd recovered from our mammoth session, Emilio and Andres told me they had an overnight trip to court, and Emilio made me a proposition.

'I need you to look after this suitcase,' he whispered. 'It has 40,000 florins [about £20,000] inside. Just make sure nobody, and I mean nobody, goes inside. We'll collect it off you when we return.'

I agreed, of course. We'd become mates in the time they'd been at La Vega.

That night we had a party in our cell, and I said to Paul, 'What about if we just take £40 out for rum? You saw the way those guys were ripping through this cash on charlie; they won't even notice it's gone.'

We picked the lock, and were greeted by huge rolls of orange and green coloured dosh – the Dutch florins. We didn't even know what the notes were worth or where Emilio had got them from; we just peeled off a few, and thought we'd taken around £50 plus a bit extra, to get it changed into local currency by the guards.

While the case was open, Paul clocked that there was a gold Breitling watch in there, and his eyes widened.

'Don't touch the watch,' I warned him. 'They're bound to notice it, and it might have sentimental value. Forget about it, brother.'

And with that, we took our rum downstairs and got wasted with our girls. By now I was seeing Siyanni and Paul was dating Kiki – the girls we'd met at the Christmas party.

Next day, Andres and Emilio came back from court and immediately went to the briefcase. Andres took one look in the case and with fury in his eyes, shouted, 'Which of you fucking bastards has taken my grandfather's watch?' It was worth £4,000 and to him it was obviously priceless.

I knew at that moment that Paul – or somebody he'd told – had taken the watch. We were in the shit. I got Paul outside and said, 'You've got five minutes to get that fucking watch back while I keep them talking.'

Back in the cell, I admitted to them I'd taken a few quid out of the case – telling them that was my price for looking after it. 'Don't be surprised we got in your case,' I said. 'This place is full of expert thieves.'

I told them I'd seen a watch in the case: 'It was gold with a blue face. But I didn't take it. I wouldn't even think about it.'

When Paul didn't come back, I went looking for him. Finally, he admitted what had happened. 'We can't get the watch back, Jim. César and me sold it for £300.'

'Shit! £300 for a £4,000 watch, you twat! We're in the shit now.'

I went to César and he gave me the brush-off. 'Chill out, Jim, they're pussies,' he said.

'Well, you go and tell them that,' I replied.

We had to take action, so I got César in the cell to admit what he'd done. But to my amazement, he said to Emilio: 'Me, Paul and Jim took your watch. The three of us did it.'

Before he could even carry on the sentence, I turned around and punched him, bawling, 'You fucking what? Shut up!', whacking him to the floor with a huge blow to his jaw. I turned to Paul and added, 'And I can't believe you went along with this and let him do it!'

Emilio, who was a big lad, said to me, 'Let me deal with this, Jim.'

But before he could act, César looked up from the floor and said to me, 'Jim, your mother is a prostitute.'

In a fit of rage, I stuck both my fingers in his eye sockets, trying to pull his eyes out. Emilio ended up pulling me off of him, and the guards sedated me – gave me a shot of something strong – to knock me out.

I'd gone mental. This wasn't good. I woke up in our cell hours later, and César was there, his bruised eyes swollen shut. But he thanked me. The Spanish gangsters had let him off. It might sound hideous, but if I hadn't taken action like that, we all could have been killed for what he did. By brutally beating the shit out of César, I'd probably saved his life.

Emilio and Andres were released soon after, and as a parting gift they offered for a Colombian cartel gang to come and blow the jail up, shoot the shit out of the place and get me out if my dad could sort them out with a bit of dough.

'But Paul can stay here and rot in hell,' they added. 'He took that fucking watch.' I shook their hands and told them while I'd be delighted if such a fate were to 'accidentally' strike La Vega at some point in the future, I wouldn't be leaving without Paul.

'He's my brother,' I told them. 'We're part and parcel. I'd never leave him behind.'

It was women that started causing real aggro for me in La Vega. Where drugs, guns, knives, violence, brutality and setting fire to people had failed, a woman was the final straw for me.

I became convinced that a prison warder was shagging my girl, got a bit jealous and got a bit aggro with him. I just wanted out, even if that meant a maximum-security prison. Even though I knew of the danger, I wanted to get out of La Vega.

We'd been locked in a cell that was twelve feet by eight feet, and apart from the odd court appearance, we hadn't seen daylight for far too long. I needed to feel the outside; I wanted to play football.

Paul was in love with Kiki and wanted to stay. He told me to chill out, but I knew the situation was killing me softly in the head.

Finally, something gave. After all the violence I'd been involved with inside, the police in La Vega started to treat me as a serious threat. They started giving me more heat, and one day they clamped down on me, confiscating my stereo for playing it too loud. I was furious – I'd bought it from them, at a massive mark-up. Admittedly it was with money I'd made from drugs, but those were all supplied by them. Plus I'd made it a mission to learn Spanish to help my chances both in nick and at court, and the radio was my teacher.

I decided one night to try and kick my way out of the place. For two hours, I kicked at a metal gate and, eventually, the bricks crumbled and the door flew off its hinges. In that moment, I realised I could have escaped. But where would I go? I didn't have a passport, and had no clue what was out there on the streets.

The guards eventually came up and just said, 'Jim's in a bad mood ...' and walked off. I pleaded with them, 'Give me my radio back, please! I'll turn it down and play salsa!', but they wouldn't. So I threw boiling water at them.

I had just wanted a reaction. By now I had no regard for my own safety, I'd just had enough. I was slowly going insane in this hellhole, and wanted out – even if it was in a straitjacket.

The female judge – the one who we reckoned looked like a prostitute – came to visit us, and asked us how it was going. I decided enough was enough; it was time to tell her the truth, no matter what the consequences.

'You wanna know how it's going here? It's all bullshit! You come here in your nice clothes, act all concerned, but you just fuck off and leave us here to rot. Nothing ever happens. This shit is killing me. I want to go to a maximum-security jail.'

Being locked up and never seeing the daylight was depressing. I'd heard that at least in proper prisons you could get out and play football. I wanted to breathe air, to see the sun and run around – even if it meant more danger.

'Are you sure about what you're saying? You know it could be very dangerous for you there. You'd be the only foreigners in the whole place ...'

'I don't care!' I screamed. 'Just fuck off, bitch!' and I turned the table over, going mental. I just wanted to wind her up, to convince her I was losing it, to provoke some action, anything.

It worked. I was put in solitary confinement for the first time. I got fifteen days. I was beaten down the corridor and shoved into a tiny concrete room on my own that was knee deep in a sewage flood: piss, shit, toilet roll, used tampons, the lot.

I was chained to the bars by my right arm, which meant it was impossible to even sit down. For three nights, I tried to sleep standing up, hanging off this bar, but I'd always wake up in agony. And if the excruciating pain didn't wake me up, the sewer rats would, as they swam past my legs in the sewage. Those slimy, bastard rats – we'd call them top hats – were the size of small dogs, with chipped, yellow teeth and hateful, beady eyes. Cockroaches were constantly crawling over my face, trying to get in my mouth or ears to lay eggs which, we were told, could grow inside your body, then rupture and spew maggots out of lumps in your neck.

After three days of this torture, I pleaded with them to let me go and unblock the toilets out in the courtyard. The bogs – just holes in the floor – were obviously blocked, and this was causing the stinking flood in my cell.

With nothing else to use, I plunged my arm into the main bog and it instantly gurgled away. My reward for that was to be let off my chain.

Added to the physical discomfort, I was starving. Paul was trying to pass me food through the bars, but every time it was intercepted.

All of this torment just made me angrier. All I'd wanted was to be moved, and my reward was this: to be treated worse than an animal, like a piece of shit. It just made me more determined.

Every day I'd plead with the guards to let me out, but they'd just smirk, 'Not until you're broken.'

I'd reply, defiantly, 'You won't ever break me, mother-fuckers.' I wanted out, but on my own terms.

After two weeks of that bollocks, they finally let me go. They only let me out because Paul's girl, Kiki, went to them crying, pleading, 'Don't you think he's had enough now?' I came out looking like Grizzly Adams, if Grizzly Adams ever dive-bombed into a giant pool of shit.

It was at this point that I tried to kill myself.

I'd always thought that suicide was for the weak, but I just couldn't see an end to it all. I necked a whole bottle of Co-codamol, but it didn't work, and Paul said to me afterwards, 'What the fuck would I do without you? Don't leave me, kid. We're in this together. I need you, Jim.'

That broke my heart. I realised that both of our lives depended on me keeping my head. I'd let both of us down, and resolved to toughen up and face the music fighting.

Paul and I were seriously close in La Vega. We were practically living in each other's pockets. Of course, we had our fallings out: at times, it seemed like we were married, and every couple has their arguments. But we loved each other like brothers.

After trying to top myself, I came to realise that to appreciate the good times, you had to go through shit. And there was plenty of that in La Vega.

Our thoughts turned to getting a new lawyer – hopefully one who wasn't crooked and who wouldn't end up murdered.

An opportunity came when my dad heard about a Dutch lad, who'd been arrested trying to smuggle one kilogram of cocaine out of Venezuela.

He had only served one month because his lawyer, a brilliant man called Jaime, had got him out.

My dad contacted Jaime. He wanted £20,000 in total, with £5,000 up front, for which he guaranteed he'd get us free. As he'd worked wonders with the other lad, my dad borrowed the cash off my grandma.

It was arranged that we could go and visit him at his offices in Caracas. When we got there, the first thing we saw was Diego – one of the cops from La Vega – leaving. I put two and two together. In a typical bit of Venezuelan intrigue, it looked like our new lawyer was in cahoots with a copper in La Vega: the perfect legal team.

Diego, who was as bent as a boomerang, had eventually become our friend in La Vega. He'd also offered to set up a real cocaine exportation operation in Venezuela on our release, saying he'd supply the drugs and bribe all the officials and get a gateway at the airport this end if we could sort the Heathrow end of the business.

It made me laugh: this was the sort of legal team we needed on our side!

Within two months, on May 15th, 1998, Jaime contacted us and said, 'That's it, you're going free. The judge is nearly ready to sign your papers; it's looking great.' He'd given us a date. Could we finally be getting out of this hellhole?

That fateful morning, about eighteen months since we'd walked into La Vega, a guard came up and said, 'Boys, that's it, you're going free today. Get your stuff together; the van from the Embassy will be here at 6 p.m.'

We were well used to these kind of wind-ups and asked him if he thought we looked like we were born yesterday. But he told us it was for real.

'Wicked!' we thought. We packed all our stuff, and at 6 p.m. we were by the gate, waiting for sweet freedom. We knew that Jaime had come to La Vega, and had delivered our release papers to the police. They had been telling us: 'We have your freedom papers here. They all seem in order. We're just finalising them with the judge. We'll ring her to make sure she's signed it.'

By 9 p.m., I was doing my nut, so demanded to know what was going on. Finally, we had our answer: 'Your papers,' said an official, calmly. 'They're not good. You two – you're fucking gangsters. You're cartel, and we're getting you out of our prison. We cannot contain prisoners like you here any longer. You are too much of a high risk.'

Not only had we not got away with it but, by trying to buy our way out of prison, the cops were now convinced we had major mob backing. They wanted to wash their hands of us.

We'd been minutes from freedom. Instead, we were now heading for a maximum-security jail.

It turned out the release form was a fake. A £5,000 fake. If the police hadn't phoned the judge, we'd have got away with it long enough to skip the country. As it turned out, that was the way the other Dutch lad we'd heard about had made it out of Venezuela.

It was another example of how absolutely everybody is out to get you once you're inside the Venezuelan prison system. We'd come close to getting freedom, we could almost taste it, but now we were going to experience something that would leave more than a bad taste in our mouth. We were on our way to South America's deadliest prison – Yare – in other words the very bowels of hell.

CHAPTER 5

DANCING WITH THE DEVIL

Yare maximum-security jail was situated in a town called San Francisco de Yare. Nicknamed '*Donde el diablo se villa*', inmates told me it translated as 'The house where the devil dances'. They could not have given it a more fitting name.

We'd arrived at Yare after travelling three hours down deserted dirt tracks in the back of a sweatbox of a van. The place was literally in the middle of nowhere. Escaping from this joint – if it was even possible – would be a seriously bad move. You could walk for days in the baking hot desert and not arrive anywhere.

The whole perimeter was surrounded by high wire fences and at regular intervals look-out towers were stationed, each manned by heavily armed National Guards.

Security was tight. When we got through the ominous iron gates, the van parked over an inspection pit, like the sort mechanics use, so the underside of our vehicle could be checked for smuggled drugs, guns or bombs. The place was thirty times the scale of anything we'd been used to: there were 3,000 inmates in there.

Both Paul and I had fallen silent. What hell would be in store here?

A truly shocking sight awaited us as we peered through into the outdoor exercise area. You could see swarms of prisoners mooching about, and even before we got out of the van you could see they were carrying guns. Guns were in their hands, sticking out of their shorts, everywhere. These prisoners were making no attempt to conceal their firearms. One of them even had grenades hanging from his belt.

While I was glad at last to be outside after such a long confinement, my first thought was: 'Shit, what kind of characters are we gonna find in here?'

The first person we met was an inmate called Malacucho. He was covered in scars, and wasted no time saying, 'Here, you will die. We will stab you today.' He spoke in Spanish, but by now we perfectly understood the language.

I replied, 'Shut the fuck up, you cock-sucking twat,' because he didn't frighten me. I was too experienced to let the first lag who saw me intimidate us. I'd seen people like him before and knew they were full of shit. I gestured to him like I was wielding a knife, and went on: 'No problem – later, we will have a knife fight.' He wasn't expecting that, and backed off. Round one to me.

They put us straight into a holding cell, where I met a guy called Carlito, who would go on to become a good acquaintance to have. By this time, I was twenty-one, and he was only eighteen, a boy, but we hit it off straight away.

Carlito had heard of us. Our reputation from La Vega had apparently preceded us, as many of our former *compadres* had been transferred here before us. 'A lot of people like you already,' he said. 'But a lot of them, they want to fuck you over.'

He told me that he'd mugged Patrick – the African prince and heroin smuggler I'd mugged in La Vega – in another jail, La Planta. The word was that Patrick wanted to murder me in revenge and was biding his time. Apparently he was building his armour up, acquiring a vast arsenal of guns, and paying guys to protect him.

I couldn't afford to be frightened by this – I had other, more immediate problems. At least Patrick wasn't in Yare, so for now, that was a battle that could wait.

Carlito told me that we wanted to get into the Annexo building: 'It's safer, a lot of corrupt ex-police are there, and you'll get an easier ride.' Pointing out of the window, he said, 'That place over there, you don't want to go in there. They call it the Tower. That place, it is shit.' He gestured over at an enormous building: a giant,

T-shaped block five storeys high. Covered in row after row of barred windows, it looked menacing, massive and forgotten. Incredibly, its decaying walls were pock-marked with bullet holes. Clearly, there'd been some serious shooting going on around here.

In between the Tower and the Annexo was an exercise yard where you could play football, volleyball and basket-ball. Around the place there were also various gyms that had been set up by groups of cons who'd welded scaf-folding bars into car wheels or buckets of dried cement. But exercise could be bad for your health, as hundreds of windows overlooked the yard – and any of them could have had armed assassins cowering in the shadows.

I was so pumped on adrenalin after our arrival, I desperately needed a spliff. Carlito made one using a page out of a Bible, which seemed fitting: religion, along with hope, was going up in smoke around here.

A few puffs in, I finally calmed down, and Carlito told me his story: 'I stab anybody in here,' he said. 'I'm the number one stabber. You want somebody stabbing, you come to me.' He also told me how he'd come to be in Yare. He had been chased onto a roof by police and fifteen cops who had all been shooting at him.

He had run out of bullets and tried to hide in a tiny gap between two houses, but the police had discovered him and opened fire from point-blank range. The bullets had passed through his chest, but he'd lived. Carlito said, 'I could feel my body bouncing off the floor, and the next thing I wake up in hospital with my mum by my side. I can't believe I survived it myself, Jim.' He showed me all his bullet-hole scars – he must have been impossible to kill. And for that reason, I wanted to make sure I stayed tight with him.

At the time, I thought Carlito was obviously a little shit; one of those bacteria you just don't want around you. But I thought the guy could also come in handy. I was new, unarmed because we'd had to make it through a full search, had no money for the same reason and, on top of everything, I was a marked man. He was a tough little crack head, a knife fight expert who had scars galore. We would go on to became great *compadres*.

Despite everything Carlito had said, I wanted to take my chances and go to live in the Tower as I didn't want the cons to think we were getting special treatment, which would make us a soft target. Over in the Tower, it was the old-fashioned Venezuelan prison industries that ruled the roost: drug dealing, robbery and selling smuggled items on the black market. It was something I knew about, that I knew I was good at. But Paul made me see sense, and we ended up in the Annexo.

As well as ex-coppers – who were in the Annexo for their own protection, having locked up lots of the lags in the Tower – there were lots of entrepreneurial types in there. One was Luis, an expert tattooist and amazing knife fighter, who was in for forgery. He had set up a tattoo business there and was so good, people visited the jail from the outside world to get inked by him, three days a week. Other men there worked, too, and made sandals, vases and other craft items, which they sold for money.

One day I asked Luis for some weed, and he said: 'Why do you do that shit? You need to have your wits about you here. Stoned people, they end up dead.'

I replied, 'I need weed to chill out. If I don't get it, I'll be shooting my gun willy-nilly off all day just to let off some steam.' I'd managed to scrape enough money together to buy a small gun by that point and Paul and I used to shoot guns in target practice to pass the time. But Luis fell silent and glared at me. 'We do not do it like that here. We have rules. Here, we fight with knives. Shoot a gun off, and you will be killed the same day. Tomorrow, I will take you to where the knife fights are held.'

He told me of another Yare rule: never touch a man's face, even in jest. It was just another macho rule, and failing to obey it would get you stabbed or shot.

I'd never met a prisoner like Luis before. I had soon found out there are three types of prisoners in jail: the poor, who would rob you blind, the 'mediocre' – middle people, who worked, got by on their wits and did their time; and then the ultra-rich bastards, who would just take from everyone. Luis belonged to the Venezuelan middle classes and was actually being nice and trying to help us. We both ended up great friends with him, and he went on to teach Paul to become an expert tattooist.

*

One of the trickiest parts of arriving in any new jail is securing a good cell. You're bottom of the pecking order, you've got no weapons and you're broke, and, unless you're prepared to fight for it, you have to take what's going.

Having a good cell isn't just about comfort or respect. It's far more important than that. Having a good, secure cell that's out of the reach of the prying eyes of the guards and thieves allows you to set up a business and stash illegal stuff where it can't be stolen or confiscated during frequent and often violent police raids.

At Yare, we got very lucky. I hooked up with a Venezuelan guy who was a professor of English, before he'd got arrested for murder, that is. He was just coming to the end of a twenty-five-year term, and had taken to us purely because we were English.

We hit it off straight away, and he promised me we could have his cell when he got out. Within days of our admission to Yare, he was released from prison and we'd bagged his room. We'd fallen straight into the right pocket. Sometimes prison is just random like that.

This cell was pukka. It was about ten feet by twelve feet, and had a big, wrought-iron gate that could be locked from the inside, meaning no fucker could steam in and rob you at night. There was also a thick metal sheet welded over the door so no nosy bastards could see in. It was like a protective bunker. Paul shared with me for a while, but for most of our stay in Yare, we had separate cells.

This cell wasn't far from the communal shower rooms either, where you'd have a wash if the water was turned on. Paul and I quickly learned that there was only one way to shower in there – with your back to the wall and a knife in your teeth. Naked and at your most vulnerable, it was important to show the others you were ready for action. We'd watch out for each other in case anybody tried to attack us. The guards rarely went in there, so there was plenty of opportunity for a quick stab in the guts.

That wasn't the only reason you didn't hang around in there. Inmates would take a dump in the open holes that passed for drains, so it stank to high heaven, and the shower itself was little more than a rusty pipe out of the wall. The water supply was just a pathetic cold dribble, so we'd fill up cut-down plastic bottles and tip those over our head instead. Taking a proper shower was just one of the many basic human rights we'd be deprived of during our time in Yare. Life's smallest pleasures just didn't exist.

* * *

'Before you go to the Tower, I need to introduce you to Chico,' said Carlito. 'He is the brains around here. Listen to him, and you might just live.' Carlito did us a good turn that day: Chico went on to become one of my protectors in Yare, and always made sure he showed his massive chrome Colt revolver when I was having a beef. But, for now, if we were to have any hope of getting out of this place alive, we had to know who controlled the prison, so Chico was an organised gang leader who was in there for countless murders and drug dealing. It was best to have him on side and he was happy to give us a master class in the complex gang structure that operated within Yare.

'There are three gangs in here,' he said. 'They're called *el Corte Negra*, *el Pollo Robo* and *el Barrio Chinos*. The Tower is split into five floors, and every floor has been commandeered by a different gang. Every gang is the sworn enemy of every other gang member. Every gang hates the other with all of his heart.'

The biggest and most respected gang in Yare was *el Corte Negra* – the Black Cut. An African gang, they controlled the ground level and level five. They practised voodoo and lots of other strange rituals. I learned that during the rituals, members became possessed by their Viking ancestors who, they believed, could predict what would happen to them. During the ceremonies, gang members were not allowed to wear black, and you couldn't cross your arms or legs during the rituals. They often contacted their Viking ancestor the night before planned knife battles or other conflicts to give help and protection.

Chico went on: 'The Black Cut are truly expert knife fighters. When they fight, they look like cobras waiting to strike. Challenge one only if you are prepared to die.' As far as I could work out, the Black Cut were like Spartans: warriors ready to scrap, and nothing else. They

weight-trained incessantly, and were also the most stylish gang there, wearing the best American clothes. They
wore New York Yankee baseball caps, had pukka Nike
Air Max trainers, the best guns, and ran all of the drug
trades. You would hear their tribe's call, which sounded
like 'Tu-tu-way!' and was their way of letting other gang
members know they were around.

To stop other gangs getting up to level five of the
Tower, they'd hooked up electric cables to the steel stairs
to stop anybody moving up or down them. If they were
concerned that someone they didn't want was about to
climb them, they'd pour buckets of water onto the live
metal, making it spit and fizz – a death sentence if you
stood on it.

The most fearsome of all the Black Cut was a vicious
psychopath they called Terminator. He looked like Mike
Tyson and only ever wore white Y-fronts, nothing else. He
had a muscle-ripped body like Ivan Drago from *Rocky IV*,
and was the prison champion for one-armed push-ups.
He was a proper, rock-hard shit head. His right-hand man
was a nutter called Punal Mortal, who was the business
head of the gang, and always demanded a slice of any
other gang's action.

Terminator's antics in gang warfare were the stuff of
legend. Terminator didn't get out much because so many
people wanted to kill him, but he used to enjoy stomping
up and down the stairs in the Tower with his Remington
pump-action shotgun, blasting off rounds into other

gangs' landing areas. He'd empty eight rounds, then go back for a refill (he had to; wearing only pants, he had nowhere to stash spare ammo). He'd kill around five inmates on each savage rampage. He was far and away one of the biggest lunatics I'd ever heard of, yet he ended up going free before we did.

Chico next told us all about Yare's second gang, *el Pollo Robo* – the Chicken Thieves. They got their unfortunate name from the fact they were rural lads, who came from the sticks. They were considered a bit dopey, and they were the scummiest of petty thieves.

They often started battles but didn't have the skill or firepower to finish them, although their weapon of choice – the *maeri braso* – was a fearsome, thin knife about half as long as an arm. They looked after levels two and four of the Tower, and wore stained, scruffy shorts, which ruled them out straight away as a mob I was prepared to take seriously.

Finally, there was *el Barrio Chinos* – the Chinese Barrier – who ruled on level three. They weren't actually Chinese, but these boys fought with machetes and used little stools they were allowed to carry around as shields. Their machetes meant they slashed rather than stabbed: they were very violent and didn't give you a chance. They were like the Japanese warriors, the Shogun, always swaggering around in gangs and looking for a fight.

Despite their fearsome reputation, they looked a bit, well, comical at first. Their uniform was long shorts and white vests with a blue bandana tied to the right arm, and a red one round their left leg. They had hair like Ronaldo at the World Cup: mostly shaved to a skinhead, but with a little tuft at the front. For some reason, they also wore Walt Disney socks – a Mickey Mouse design was a favourite – and sprinkled baby talc on their shoulders. Christ knows why; it was just one of their marks. They'd let you know they were around by chanting, 'Ya-hooo!', which made them sound like packs of hyenas.

But you'd be insane to laugh at them, even when they were old enough to be your dad, as old as forty (an age most cons didn't see), and they still dressed that way; because, on top of it all, they had the biggest stash of the most fearsome weapon money could buy in Yare: hand grenades, which they'd parade around, showing off, at every opportunity.

What Chico was telling us was by equal measures price-less and terrifying. Remember that first day at big school, when you turned up and had no idea what the big lads might do to you? What's the worst that could have happened? Some kid might have nicked your dinner money, right?

Now take that fear and multiply it by a million. Only instead of there being some gang of older lads who might take the piss out of you for wearing crap trainers, there are instead 3,000 drugged-up psychopaths, armed to the teeth with blades, shooters and bombs. That's the only way I can describe Yare. It was a murderous viper's nest of assassins, cut-throats and killers.

* * *

Between the Annexo and the Tower was an open piece of land meant for exercise. The problem was, all of the windows from the Tower looked down on it, meaning there could be literally hundreds of guns pointing at you at any one time. To go out there, you couldn't have any unresolved beefs with anybody or you might easily cop a bullet in the back of the head.

Paul and I had only been at Yare for two days when we witnessed an example of this with our own eyes. It was 8 a.m., but it was a red-hot morning already. Paul and I were standing in the queue at the kitchen waiting for some breakfast, when a Black Cut gang member turned to us and said, 'You *gringos* ever seen anybody get killed before?'

Shocked, Paul said, 'Erm, no, why?'

Smiling, the gang member had replied, 'Well, you will today, *amigos*.'

A kid in a checked shirt had walked out of the Tower and joined the queue, about two or three people behind us.

At that moment, we caught a movement out of the corner of our eyes: a bloke from the Black Cut, in shorts, ran out from behind a corner, put a gun right to the kid's head and *bang!*, pulled the trigger.

He was packing a .357 Magnum, which anybody knows is a serious bit of kit. The kid flew about three feet off the ground before he even touched the floor, his head blown clean apart. You could see a mist of blood coming out of his head.

Paul was going, 'Shit! Shit! Shit!' This was like something out of *Goodfellas*; an assassination in broad daylight. This poor lad was lying on the floor, brains all over the place, his body jerking like a fish out of water, while his assassin ran off and vanished before anybody even noticed. It was the first death, the first cold-blooded killing, we'd ever seen. Our ears were ringing from the gunfire, which had only been five or six yards from us.

We were absolutely overcome by a paralysing terror. All I could think was, 'Shit, this place is more serious than anywhere we've ever been before in our lives.' Nothing can steel you for sights like that. This wasn't a movie. This was reality.

I suddenly realised at that point that I wasn't a serious hard man. I'd had a few scuffles and dished out a few punishments, but I knew I wasn't capable of a horrible, cold-blooded drop like that. It scared me. Likewise, Paul was shocked to his core by it, too. Who could blame him?

It made me wonder if that killer had always been mad like that, or had this place sent him that way? And what would it do to us?

I knew I'd already been changed by my time in jail, and I now really started to worry it might get worse. Were we even in control?

'Where is this place going to take us?' I said to Paul, who just looked back at me, stunned.

One week into our stay at Yare, we made the decision to carry on where we left off at La Vega, and set up as drug dealers.

It had become pretty obvious that in order to survive this place we would need to have knives and guns, and we'd never be able to afford them by dicking around making sandals or cleaning cells.

We employed Carlito as our enforcer. Any drug distribution outfit needs a ruthless member who is prepared to seriously rough up non-payers at the drop of the hat. With Carlito's history and reputation, he was the perfect man for the job.

Every month, my dad would send me some money over, usually about £30 to £50. You might think that kind of dosh would be a lot of money in Yare, but it didn't last five minutes in there. Everybody would know we'd been sent money because to receive it we would have an Embassy visit. Once a month, the British Consulate rep would come in and give us legal updates, and pass us the cash from back home. As all the other inmates knew what was going on, they'd want our money off us the second we came out.

So, as soon as our first lot of money from our families came in from our Embassy official, I was buying cocaine from bent guards to cook into crack. Paul was a genius at it. The right ratio was fifty grams of coke to eight grams of baking soda. We'd put the mix in a baby food jar, then place it in a pan of boiling water and cook it on the stove. Other times we just lit a candle under it and left it bubbling. Once it was cooked, you'd add water until it just covered the mix. When an oily residue appeared on the surface, Paul would plunge the jar into a vat of ice. At that point, it would crystallise – and crack the jar as it expanded, hence the name.

Our new network worked really well: we got £50 each from our parents every month, and instantly invested, say, £30 of it into cocaine. Coke in Yare was about £2 a gram, which was a bit pricier than in La Vega – this isolated jail was forty miles from Caracas, meaning it was harder to get deliveries. But for £30 we'd still get fifteen grams of cocaine – ninety per cent pure – from the guards (the stuff on British streets has been cut down with God knows what before it gets to the user, and weighs in at as low as ten or fifteen per cent cocaine content).

We'd triple our money on this stuff. So our £30 became £90, which allowed us to buy even more cocaine the next time, plus we set money aside for other essentials, like weapons. This stopped the other gangs that controlled the drug trade from becoming pissed off that we were stepping on their toes, as the money we earned on drugs we'd spend on weapons and other drugs from them.

*

Food for a month only cost us a fiver. There was food provided there – if you got to it – but who fancied boiled whole sardines in flavourless rice and endless luncheon meat?

The prison kitchen used to cook a dish called *sambumbia* once every three days: a giant metal pot filled with chicken knuckles, rice and any old cheap crap they could lay their hands on. This pot went around five other local police stations before it got to us, so we just got the shit nobody else wanted – bones and slops. We'd seen guards hawk greenies into it before, too, so unless you were the very poorest of the poor, you'd avoid it like the plague. Even then, you'd have to cook it again to kill off the germs and avoid a serious dose of the trots.

Getting your hands on clean water was also a problem. In desert-surrounded Yare, the water would only be switched on for a few hours every couple of days. We'd hoard as many empty water bottles as we could and wait for the guards to bellow '*Aqua!*' through their megaphones, then we'd stampede to the water points with as many containers as we could carry.

It made us feel like we were in the middle of some Live Aid-type famine in Ethiopia. Grown men would pull knives, throw punches, kick and bite like animals, just to get at the water ahead of somebody else. If somebody shoved in front of someone, then the supply was cut off, and vicious fights would erupt. It was another way of making our behaviour descend into that of animals.

Bad water was a killer. The results of it was way beyond getting a bad dose of the trots after a dodgy curry, or something to laugh about with the boys in Benidorm. We'd regularly see perfectly healthy men die of terrible, convulsive fevers brought on by dysentery or cholera from dirty water. These guys would literally shit their lives out of their arses. The guards just let them shiver and wither away if they couldn't afford a doctor or medicine. To them, it was just one less mouth to feed.

To avoid having to eat prison food, with our profits we'd buy a job lot of rice, pasta, tomato sauce, eggs, butter and a few veggies. By this time, we both loved Venezuelan food, and cooked it ourselves for most meals. It was also loads better value. White bread out there cost a fortune, as it had to be imported. You'd be talking £1 for that, whereas ham was 15p a pack and it was 6p for milk. So a loaf of bread was the same price as a gram of cocaine, a packet of cigs or a small flask of rum! You could pick up two litres of vodka for £4 – a guard would smuggle it in in a fruit juice carton.

A favourite dish was called an *arepa*, which was ground-cornflour patties. Known as 'dominoes' because of the black spots that appeared on them while they cooked, you would fry or grill them and stuff them with whatever you had, like black beans with white cheese and butter. Then there were *empanadas*, which are a Venezuelan version of Cornish pasties, stuffed with grated beef and peppers.

*

Better food was a luxury, but it was a drop in the ocean towards making us feel better about where we were. I got into tranquillisers, like Diazepam, which I'd use as anti-depressants, as did a lot of people in there, who walked around in a trance, like zombies.

Paul was also sniffing a serious amount of coke. He'd sniff all night and sleep all day, and more than once I'd had to warn him to cut down on the amount he was taking. I tried to get him to come outside and play foot-ball, but he had little interest. Drugs were becoming a big – if not the biggest – part of our lives. They were the only chance of escape from the relentless stress and terror of living where we were. But it was business as usual, too – we had to stay on top, be someone in there, to have any chance of surviving to our let-out date.

If anybody didn't pay us for drugs, we'd send Carlito after them. He didn't give a fuck about anybody. He'd challenge people to a knife fight over a fifty-pence debt. He'd say, 'OK, no problem, you took our drugs, you refuse to pay. I will forget about the money if you will knife fight with me to settle our score.' Carlito had had scores of knife fights and was unbeaten. He was so good at knife fighting, in fact, that his threats usually did the trick and the person would pay up.

If they still refused to pay, he'd give them a warning and stab them in the leg. Carlito didn't own a gun – he couldn't afford one – but he never wanted to borrow one to put the shit up people or to protect himself. He was old-fashioned, and always wanted to do business with his knife.

Carlito would come back and report to me, and I'd reward him with crack to feed his own addiction. Everybody was happy.

Carlito also looked after a black guy called Deon, a cocaine trafficker, who eventually moved into my cell. Deon was a good guy and I really took to him. But he went a bit doolally when he heard his girlfriend was having an abortion against his will; he really got into the crack and started losing it. In the end, he got 'possessed by a demon' and it fucked him right up.

I knew things were in a bad way when I got to my cell one night, and there was a crucifix on my door; only it was upside down. I'm not a religious person, so I took it off and threw it on the floor. I booted my cell door open, and Deon was sitting on the floor, naked, reading the Bible, which was also upside down. He sounded like he was reading it backwards; he was making these weird, deep, demonic, almost animal noises, like when you hear a record being played backwards. It totally freaked me out.

Before I could say anything, he took some ammonia we'd got in the cell for cooking crack, and he started spraying it on my feet. I was wearing flip flops, and that shit burns your skin straight away on contact. This was getting out of hand.

I jumped backwards, shouting, 'What the fuck are you doing?', and he replied, 'You have the devil in you! The devil is where you walk in this room!'

He was chewing a bar of soap and foaming at the mouth. In short, he'd gone totally fucking loopy. We had to drag him out of the room and slap him into shape, because he was going downhill. In the end, he did make it back. But, like many people, the madness of Yare had almost totally taken over his mind.

* * *

The trouble with being top of the tree inside a jail like Yare is that somebody always wants to kill you. They've either got a beef with you about something from the past, or they just want to take you out to improve their own standing.

Even though the Black Cut practically ran Yare, it was just too dangerous for them to walk around in the exercise yard, as there'd always be some nutter willing to take a pot-shot at them. It happened to my mate, Joseph; a Black Cut who ended up getting killed when he went for a jog around the exercise yard. Somebody hiding in a bush fired off a round and Joseph got a bullet through the head, just because he wanted to go and take some exercise.

I like a jog as much as the next man, but I wasn't prepared to die for one.

So it was no wonder they got up to all sorts of crap in the Tower – it was probably boredom as much as anything else.

But *el Barrio Chinos*, they didn't give a fuck. They walked around bold as brass, thanks to their hand grenades. They called them *pina* – Spanish for pineapples. You could get them easily enough if you had a spare £20 – the price of a decent round of drinks back home. They were green, ex-WWII British numbers, and God knows where they got them from.

I saw at least two go off during my time in Yare. They left a big pit in the ground, about three feet deep, with a five-metre radius. Those grenades definitely weren't props. They were the real deal. Madness.

One day, a lad from *el Barrio Chinos*, who was wanted by Terminator, got a visit from his mum and his girlfriend. There was such a price on this guy's head, he hadn't been outside the Tower in over two years. But the day his mum and girlfriend turned up to see him in the Tower, he decided it was worth finally breaking his exile and going outside for some fresh air. Of course, everybody got to hear about this, and guys from the Black Cut were queuing up to kill him.

When he finally emerged from the Tower, however, he had one arm round his mum, the other round his missus, and he had a grenade in his right hand, on his mum's shoulder, with the pin in his mouth. He had the pin out of the *pina*! It was the craziest thing I'd ever seen in my life.

The grenade would have been on a three-second fuse, so it was pretty obvious that if anybody wanted to take a shot at him, he would drop the grenade – and take out whoever was near him, including his mum and girl-friend. He took the pin out of his mouth and started screaming: 'Any of you motherfuckers come near me and we're all fucking going up! Stay away from me, cos I want some fucking space!'

He kept chanting: 'I'm willing to kill us all!' I wasn't that bothered if he wanted to kill his mum and his girlfriend – that was his stupid choice – but even in Venezuelan jails, there aren't that many nutters who would be willing to have the blood of two innocent women on their hands. Plus, the retribution for such an attack would have been unspeakable. It would have led to all-out warfare. For once, Terminator had to bite his lip and let this guy live.

* * *

As Brits, we had the option to join any of the gangs in Yare, and we opted to align with the Black Cut. You had to be connected: there was strength and protection in unity. I chose them because I felt secure with them. I liked their ways, and they were stylish. They were cocky and smoked weed, whereas the other gangs were high on crack, and wasting themselves away with it. I liked their clothes, they ate good food, and their girlfriends were fit – as were their sisters! They also had access to the best drugs and guns, which helped.

There was some serious firepower in Yare. We'd seen nothing on this scale in La Vega. Everybody who could afford a gun owned one, and if you couldn't afford one, you could borrow money and get one on tick – although not paying back a gangster who's packing a gun and high on drugs is never a good idea.

We knew we had to get a gun if we were going to survive. The first gun I bought was a pen gun, like some gadget a spy would have – real James Bond shit. We had got close to a guy called Ayala, who worked in the prison's electricity sub-station, as his girlfriend wanted him to learn English. We'd teach him while playing cards under a mango tree in the yard. We got on well, and only about two weeks into our stay at Yare, he said to us, 'You two, you need a gun. Check this out. You can have it for £20.'

It looked like a normal metal pen, like a Parker pen, silver with a gold tip, only it had one .22 bullet inside it. The one drawback was that there was no safety catch on it, so it was definitely not the sort of pen you'd want to leave in your trousers pointing at your bollocks.

Ayala went on, 'This gun, it is only for killing. It is not for wounding. Use it only when you don't want some motherfucker to come back at you.' He looked at me to check I was listening. 'To kill somebody with it, go up to them, put your arm around their neck, place the tip in the soft part under the jaw and operate it by pulling the top back and letting it snap down onto the firing pin. *Boom*, it will blow out the top of their head. The .22 bullet might be small, but it is very dangerous in the right gun.'

I shot it at a wall to see how it felt. It was quite loud and you felt it kick all right. But it was a bit of a comedy gun, to be honest – you could hardly put your arm round a guy's neck and operate a fucking pen in the middle of a face-off.

A couple of months later, I traded up and, via a corrupt guard I bribed, acquired a Walther PPK. It was a proper German gun.

It cost £250, and I borrowed the money off *el Courte Negra*. I paid them back a week later with £300 (those were the terms) I'd borrowed from my dad. I didn't tell him what the loan was for. It was just too dangerous in Yare not to carry one.

The gun was chrome, with a wooden handle. I had approached a corrupt guard and said to him outright, 'Look, I need a gun, can you help?' I had known he'd be up for it, as he was my main supplier of weed (getting drugs off the Black Cut was too unreliable, as they'd be on lockdown so often for misbehaving. In a lockdown scenario, nobody was allowed in or out of the Tower, leaving the rest of us drug-free, bored and clucking for a smoke).

When I'd taken that first kilo of weed off him, the guard asked, 'Do you want anything else from me, *amigo*? Anything you want. Money talks in this place. If you've got the money, I'll get you whatever you want.'

'Fine,' I'd said, 'get me a gun.' I had been pumping with adrenalin as I'd asked. This was a make or break moment as, in principle, it was a serious offence to bribe a guard, and an even bigger offence to own a gun.

I was mightily relieved when he replied, 'Sure. Do you want a big gun, or a little gun?'

'I want a little gun,' I'd said. 'One I can conceal in my waistband, and one that's easy to hide from prying eyes and thieves.'

'What about a Glock?' he suggested. 'You know, an FBI gun. It's small, light and because it's made of plastic, it floats in water, and you can smuggle it through airport security.'

I'd kept my tone jokey – 'What are you on about? We're not going anywhere near any fucking airport for some time! Just get me a little gun!' – but all the time I was thinking what a stupid tosser he was. When did he think we were going near an airport?

By this time, we'd given up caring about when we were going to get out of jail and back to England. There just didn't seem to be any point. Every time we got our hopes up, they were just crushed by another agonising legal twist. Two days later, the guard smuggled in the wooden handle of the gun for me to look at. It didn't look a bad size, so I agreed to the sale going ahead. He then brought in the barrel and the pin, and finally the magazine. The guard showed me how to clip it together piece by piece, and I was armed and ready for action.

I asked about the ammo: 'There're only seven bullets in here – I'll let those off in one rip.' A sock of bullets – which contained about seventy slugs – set me back a further £60.

I worked out that it was about eighty pence to kill a man.

The gun was so small, you could hide it in your sock and just whip it out. This meant you could keep your main gun in the waistband of your shorts, but keep the PPK hidden. It was the dream team. It was a great second gun to have stashed about you. Even if some arsehole made you surrender your main shooter by pulling their gun on you first, you could still pull that gun out of your sock and stick it between their eyes, saying, 'Give me my fucking gun back!'

It got me out of a lot of tight corners in the time I was in Yare. I'm not making out it was a special gun – Paul always said that PPKs were as 'common as dog shit' in Yare. But to me it was a lifeline, and precious. I soon realised, however, that the 7mm bullets the PPK took were hard to get and more expensive, so I traded up to a Beretta 9mm three months later. But I always kept the PPK. I loved that little gun; it was my favourite of all the guns I had in my time in jail.

The Beretta was chrome and just looked the nuts. It was common to own bling guns, to impress and intimidate others, and the Baretta was mine. It had cost £400, which was a lot of dosh.

It was so shiny, it got you noticed, but I'd been warned that it could easily jam in warfare, and that could get me killed. Nobody wants their gun jamming if you drop it in a scuffle or knock it against a wall, and to be honest it felt like a bit of a liability. I'd always thought Berettas were brilliant – and so did Paul, who also bought one – because you see them in *Goodfellas*, but they were called 'Italian shit' by the top boys in Yare. Basically, the Beretta is a sports gun, not a hunting gun, and just can't be trusted.

Eventually, I got a Browning pistol, a proper combat gun for use in the battlefield. You could lie a foot deep in shit with that thing, get it out and it would go, no questions asked. It was the best £200 I ever spent.

I'd heard there was an Uzi in Yare, which I could well believe because the guards had them, and anything a guard owned would be for sale at the right price. I knew there was a Rem shotgun, because you could hear it every time Terminator got agitated and went on another killing spree. There were also plenty of Glocks, both 17s and 19s.

Even though we saw Mac-10 machine pistols – like the weapons you get in *Grand Theft Auto* – and even a Kalashnikov assault rifle, the daddy of all shooters in Yare was a Desert Eagle as seen in *Robocop*. This is a gas-powered semi-automatic pistol, the absolute don. There's a switch on them that allows you to have it set on one shot, semi-automatic or fully auto, so it went 'Doof', 'Doof-doof!' or 'Doof-doof-doof-doof!' until the clip was empty – and it held twenty-two bullets. Can you imagine that coming at you? When the guards heard that gun going off in automatic mode, that's when they shit themselves.

There was one chrome Smyth and Wesson .357 Magnum in Yare, too, with the hexagonal barrel and a rubber handle. That's one big gun. Paul and I both got to hold it, as it belonged to my mate, Joseph, the one who got shot when he went for a jog. We had to hold it with two hands, it was so huge. I just thought, 'Fucking hell, how does Clint Eastwood shoot one of these bastards?'

But by far the scariest and most gruesome guns in the whole place were the homemade affairs, which were placed at the entrance to every gang's landing inside the Tower.

They were fearsome, DIY guns, made from one- or even two-metre-long scaffolding poles. Inside these, they'd place five shotgun cartridges on which they'd unpeeled the tips, shaken the ball bearings out, then replaced them with nasty stuff like rusty screws and glass, before sealing them up again. For good measure, they'd tip some mercury in, too, which is a deadly poison if it gets in your bloodstream. For the firing pin, they hit five nails through a perfectly drilled metal disc, then held them in place inside the scaff pole with melted-down plastic obtained from milk containers. This created five firing pins, and meant that all five cartridges would go off at exactly the same time. The 'trigger' was a length of elastic bungee cable, which they'd pull back and let go, at which point there was a deafening *boom*.

Primitive, yes. Ingenious, yes. Effective, you bet.

These guns shot for half a mile and were called *chupa kabra*s – cow droppers. Their owners would often joke that one of those guns could blow a bull clean out a field, so you could only imagine what they could do to a man. The rumour had it that if you put eight men in front of a cow dropper, at ten feet away, it would chop them all in half. Apparently, when the mercury is travelling that fast, even though it's a liquid metal, it will still rip holes in someone because it's so dense.

Mercury was also used in regular bullets. They'd saw a cross on the tip of a bullet, making it into a dum-dum (a bullet that expands or 'ruptures' when entering its target, for maximum damage), then pour mercury in and seal it with candle wax. It was designed purely to kill.

The cow dropper really was one of the nastiest things I think I've ever known a man to invent. But at least you didn't hear them go off very often. They were the ultimate deterrent, Yare's version of a nuclear bomb. Nobody wanted to tangle with a cow dropper. So they had the effect of keeping a gang's floors reasonably secure from invasions from other gangs. And even if you were mad, angry or drugged-up enough to take on the cow dropper, on top of that, there were usually five upturned beds blocking the way into every landing area, plus a guard armed to the teeth, with guns behind every single door.

The message was clear: if you wanted to try and take another gang's floor, you had better be prepared for lots of your men to die in agony.

I also got a look at the kind of pain homemade guns can inflict when a new lad called Al Kemid turned up. He was in for multiple murder. His brother owned a jeans shop in a little village, and three men had come in and robbed him. He wasn't a violent man, so let them get away with it, but the shame was too much for Al Kemid. As the robbers had only been able to carry away half of his brother's stock, the next day Al Kemid had waited for them to come back, sitting behind the counter with two Beretta 9mm pistols. Sure enough, the three thieves had walked back in. Al Kemid had chased them down the road, and shot all three dead on the high street in front of everybody. Because he owned up to it immediately, he only got eight months. No paperwork, no trial; just get in and get out. He was fucking brilliant, and we became mates.

Not long after he'd arrived, he turned to me and said, 'Jim, we need a shooter.' He showed me how to fabricate a homemade shotgun, which we called our 'spreader'. I sorted out the cartridges, firing pin and scaffolding pipe, and it took us two days to make. I'd thought over the implications, however, and said to him, 'No way am I stashing that in my cell. If they catch a *gringo* with it, they're gonna want lots of bribe money to keep it quiet. I'll help you make the gun, but you can hide it in your cell.'

One day, Al Kemid was shooting off a few rounds in his cell to impress his mates, when a search kicked off. In his panic, Al Kemid stuffed the gun inside one of his bed poles, which were welded-together lengths of scaffolding pole. It fitted in with the barrel facing downwards, but the trigger end was still poking out, so he draped a blanket over it.

When the guards came in, acting innocent, he got on his bed to lie down – and the gun went off. It blew the scaff pole apart, lifting the bed clean off the floor. It also blew Al Kemid's leg to shit, filling it full of shrapnel. He was pouring blood, and screaming his head off.

Of course, the guards wouldn't let him see a doctor, and pretty soon the leg was badly infected. He used to drink a bottle of rum and bite on a blanket while squeezing shrapnel out of his leg – along with lots of green and yellow pus. It used to stink, and I was amazed he didn't have to have it amputated.

Al Kemid also had a huge sexual appetite, which he sorted by getting a group of new guards in his pocket, via an elaborate system of bribes. From then on, a taxi full of whores would turn up from Caracas weekly; three were for the inmates, and two for the guards. He was also dead clever. He noticed early on that a lot of people got the munchies after smoking puff, so he set up a tuck shop. 'The first rule of business, Jim, is to know your market.' He made vanilla milkshakes with dark chocolate fudge that just tasted proper when you were stoned. The guy even made knickerbocker glories! He had a queue of stoners most nights, and I'd spend £50 in one month alone.

It made me realise that even in the grimmest places on earth, there were some good people and some sort of escape to be had. In those sorts of places you could either laugh or cry, and blokes like Al Kemid helped you smile.

CHAPTER 6
ANGELS AND DEMONS

Words cannot describe how much Paul meant to me. We had been in this hell together for over two crazy years now and I would have died for him, and I knew the feeling was mutual. We were stronger together and we both said, on many occasions, that we would never have made it without each other.

More than that, you only realise how important people are to you when their life is in danger.

In Yare, we used to have situations called 'red light' and 'green light'. Basically, if there'd been some heavy shit going down, you could feel the atmosphere instinctively. You knew not to go out into open air. There'd be guns at windows, bullets bouncing off walls and no guards would even dare to try and stop it. That was a red light situation.

On one such occasion, Paul was gagging for some weed and decided to go to the Tower. For once, the trouble seemed to be elsewhere, so he thought it would be fine. He got there uneventfully, scored some puff and was on his way back, when suddenly, a bunch of guards with guns appeared around the perimeter of the yard and just let rip.

During lockdowns, it was Yare law that the guards were allowed to open fire on anybody who went into the yard. Paul could hear the bullets going 'Ping, ping, ping!' as they ricocheted off walls all around him and knew he had to get out of there. He had his Beretta with him, and pulled it, spraying the whole clip back towards the windows where the guards were, to give him some cover while he legged it back into the Annexo. He ended up hiding under a set of stairs, crying his eyes out.

I'd heard the commotion and went ballistic. 'Where the fuck have you been? Don't ever do that again! Are you mad?' I screamed. I was angry not because of what he'd done, but because he almost got killed. I couldn't imagine a life without Paul. We were in this together.

Then, a few weeks later, Paul developed a bad cough. Even though we tried to brush it off as too many spliffs, it wouldn't go away. Of course, the guards didn't give a rat's arse about it, but it worsened, so we complained to the Embassy.

It really got to me. Paul was my brother, yet he was in pain and I couldn't do anything about it. I started having crazy thoughts about him dying. I couldn't imagine a life without him. We'd been through so much shit together, and I loved the fella to pieces. We needed each other to survive.

Paul's weight plummeted from twelve to nine and a half stone in just two weeks. He was coughing up blood every minute he was awake and had a terrible, deathly fever.

Despite this, Yare's authorities wouldn't take him to hospital or even get a doctor in. Instead, he had to spit in a jam jar and they sent it off to a laboratory for testing.

After an agonising week's wait, we finally discovered that Paul had contracted tuberculosis. In Britain, that sort of crap went out with the Victorians, but in Venezuelan jails, it was way too common – and if you couldn't afford a doctor, it was a killer. We'd seen inmates too poor to afford treatment die from its agonising cough and fever.

Once again, the Venezuelan cons turned to DIY medicine. They boiled up carrots, then poured a pint of orange juice in to the water to give Paul a vitamin boost. That was when you saw good in these people. They all pulled together to help Paul, and it meant the world to us.

Even though we were surrounded by killers, it made us see that truly there is good in everyone, if you look hard enough.

Eventually, the Embassy sent through some giant pills, and after three weeks of illness Paul was on the mend. He'd made it. They say that what doesn't kill you makes you stronger; Paul's TB certainly made our bond of friendship and brotherhood that little bit more special.

Violence was so commonplace in Yare, most of the time the guards couldn't even be arsed to come and break it up. Unless it got properly serious, they'd just carry on playing cards, smoking, scratching their balls and watching shite soap operas on their crappy little tellies.

Every single day we were there we'd see physical violence of some sort. Five or six guys were getting killed every week, but as far as the cops were concerned, that was five or six fewer inmates to worry about, and six bullets they'd saved – the National Guard were legally allowed to shoot anybody dead who went out at night, or stepped over a yellow exclusion line painted around the perimeter fence. Their attitude was to let the prison police itself, unless things got too out of hand, at which point they'd come down on us like a ton of bricks and start blasting their shotguns and pumping CS gas around like it was air freshener.

The more sadistic guards also liked to dish out a good, physical beating every now and then. In fact, the guards used to routinely challenge the inmates to fights at organised boxing nights, apparently to boost morale.

Word had got out that the governor of the place wanted to fight one of the English lads, because he knew we'd invented the sport. He was quite an old boy, and I asked him if he was sure, as I'd been boxing all the time

I was in jail to keep me fit and sane, and had got quite good at it, but he was insistent.

There was no way I was going to let this old ponce do me over, especially as the entire prison had turned up to watch. Well, as soon as the bell rang for the start of round one, this old cunt came at me, throwing a fancy one-two combination. I just stepped back, thought, 'Fuck off!', and sent a fierce jab right into his nose. I felt his schnozzer go right into my glove; it made a sickening crack and I knew I'd flattened it.

Sure enough, his hooter was all over his face, there was blood everywhere and I got this huge round of applause from the inmates. I thought I was in deep shit, with solitary confinement and knee-deep sewage for tea, no doubt. But the governor just came over and shook my hand. Fair fight and all that.

It made me think, though. If the head honcho shook your hand for flattening his nose, he wasn't going to give a shit about what the inmates did to each other, was he? I wondered how far you could go before you actually got told off. I'd soon get the chance to find out.

One particularly evil and hateful inmate was a seventeen-stone Colombian body-builder we nicknamed Seven Necks. He'd taken so many steroids and pumped so much iron, there were so many ripples of muscles in his neck, it looked like he had seven necks in one.

He had a huge scar from a machete wound that ran right down the centre of his chest and made him look like he'd been opened up. Over the top of this horrible scar was a massive tattoo of a scorpion. All the messages he sent out were 'fuck with me at your peril'.

Seven Necks was the governor's chef and a terrible, terrible bully. He once beat the shit out of his cell mate, Fats, in full view of everybody, simply because Fats had failed to wake him for roll call. It didn't matter to Seven Necks that he'd been up all night taking crack and wanking off to porn, meaning he'd slept through. For this lie-in, Seven Necks had got his arse beaten with a sword, and he took his revenge out on poor Fats. Seven Necks knew Fats wasn't a fighter, he just did it to humiliate him.

He wouldn't do that to the tougher guys, though, because he knew they'd stick up for themselves. And therein lies the rub: if you don't stand up to arseholes like Seven Necks in jail, they will fuck you over, bully you and make your life hell every single day.

I hate bullies, and I really hated Seven Necks.

While Seven Necks might have scared grown men, he hadn't banked on the fearless local insect called the botfly. We'd heard of these insects before. These flies travel on mosquitoes or horseflies and, while the mozzy feeds, lay their eggs on the person's skin. Woken by body heat the eggs hatch, and the little larvae burrow into your skin, and start to feed. Rumour had it that if they got into people's ears, they could hear them munching away, something that had sent men so insane that they had cut their ears open with knives to get them out.

One day, playing cards under the mango tree in the yard, I noticed a black insect land on the top of my nose, near my eye. I batted it away and thought no more of it until later that night, when it began itching like buggery. I felt this little lump, like gristle, under the skin, squeezed it for a bit, but forgot about it.

The next day, my eye was shut tight, like there was a sty there, and it hurt to blink. Come the afternoon, and it looked like I had a nipple growing out of my face. Other lads were getting them everywhere, too: under their arms, on their legs, round their bollocks and even up their arses. Word spread that we'd all been hit by a plague of botflies, which meant we all had maggots growing inside us.

About a week and a half later, I was playing cards again when I saw this white grub wriggling out of the corner of my eye. I said to Ayala, 'For fuck's sake, squeeze it out!' He grabbed it by its arse, and yanked it out. There it was: an inch-long, wriggling maggot covered in custard-coloured pus. I had a hole in the side of my nose where the bastard had been living, in its little maggot's cave, feasting off my living flesh.

But even in this cruel world, there was proof of a God – Seven Necks ended up with eight of the little fuck-ers burrowing in around his ball sac. He had to suffer the indignity of lying on his back with his legs pulled back and his bollocks round his ears, while some poor sod squeezed the maggots out, one by one. Everybody in the cell block could hear Seven Necks screaming his tits off – while we were laughing off ours.

But then Seven Necks beat up Paul and I knew he had to suffer some more. Nobody hurt my brother.

He shared a cell with us for a time. The guards had moved him in and we didn't like him, he didn't like us, and our beef just started from there. He'd stay awake all night watching porn and masturbating while we tried to sleep. It was severely unfunny and Paul, who was much more mild-mannered than me, was at breaking point with the guy.

Seven Necks was the type of prat who'd shout at you, then punch the wall until it rocked. When he did this to us one day, I'd had enough, and just wanted to shut him up, so I clouted the wall myself, and shouted, 'Any fucker can hit a wall! Walls don't hit back!'

He had glowered at me, but walked off. Major tension was brewing between us, and it would only be a matter of time before it kicked off. He knew it, I knew it – every bugger knew it.

Rumours started going round that I was 'going to give it to Seven Necks, English style'. Sure enough, that night, I heard our pal Edmundo in the next cell saying, 'Have you ever seen that English film called *Scum*? The English don't fuck about – they put pool balls in socks and smash it straight round a man's head and knock him out. Seven Necks isn't nothing compared to what Jim could do.'

I could hear him bigging me up as everybody laughed, and I knew I would have to kick it off soon, or I'd be seen as a bottler. So many beefs start that way, with idle talk, and the next thing you know you just have to step up and do the business, even if you don't really want to.

The final straw came one afternoon when Seven Necks smashed Paul in the face for no reason whatsoever, cutting Paul's lips and busting his nose. When Paul got back to our cell, he was livid, crying with anger. That really got to me. Nobody could do that to my brother and get away with it.

Paul began frantically trying to find a big piece of wood with nails in it he had, to smash Seven Necks with.

I asked, 'Are you telling me Seven Necks smacked you in the mouth for no reason at all?' And when he replied, 'Yeah, I was just standing there minding my own business. I'm gonna do him in, I've had enough of him bullying me,' that was it. I saw red. This bullying had to stop.

'You're not smashing Seven Necks in the head,' I said. 'I am.'

We had a big brass doorknob on our cell door. I'd been eyeing it up for a while as a potential weapon, so I quickly unscrewed it. To my amazement, it weighed about four bloody kilos. It was a beast. I lobbed it inside two football socks, then tucked it inside the big, baggy pair of shorts I was wearing, to hide it. Tying it round a belt loop, so that it was hanging next to my knackers,

I steamed out into the yard, Paul right behind me, to where Seven Necks was standing.

He was armed with a short length of scaffolding pole and a knife. He smiled. 'I've been waiting for you, *gringo*.'

I said, 'Have you, you cunt? What did you hit my brother for?'

He replied, 'Fuck your brother!' Mistake. Say what you like about me, but leave Paul out of it.

I yanked the doorknob out of my shorts by the sock, and swung it at his giant head. But as I started swinging, he ducked and came at me with the scaff bar and knife. Luckily, however, the doorknob looped over his head, the football socks stretched round his dome and the huge lump of brass hit him on the back of his chest with an almighty, sickening thud. Paul told me after it was the worst noise he'd ever heard.

Seven Neck's eyes rolled back in his skull. I'd hit his lung or something, and he was giving it all – his arms flapped; the bar dropped from his hand, the knife from the other.

I booted him with a fly kick straight in his chest, and he gasped and went down. I should have stopped, but rage was coursing through me. I got him straight in a head lock, and was punching him in his dome, when Paul decided he wanted to hit him too, and swung a boot into Seven Neck's bollocks like Jonny Wilkinson converting a try.

Adrenalin was surging round my body by this time,

and I shoved Paul off, shouting, 'You've had your chance! He's mine now, so fuck off!' In the distraction, Seven Necks sank his teeth into my left thumb, instantly going down to the bone. He was gnawing on it, making horrible, savage noises like a pitbull terrier. I was smacking him in the ear, trying to make him let go, but he wouldn't. If I didn't take action, Seven Necks was going to bite my thumb clean off.

Screaming obscenities, I found myself ramming the strongest fingers on my right hand into his eye sockets. My fingers went right behind his eyeballs, and I felt his eyes pop. I *heard* them pop.

Seven Necks groaned and finally let go of my thumb. Blood was pissing out of it. As a last measure, I stamped hard on his head in a fit of pain and rage.

By now, the guards had heard the fight and were pouring out of their quarters with shotguns. They ordinarily might not have cared, but as Seven Necks was connected to the governor, they rushed to his defence. 'Off him!' they bellowed, and sent a few rounds off into the air. It was time to stop.

I tried to act as innocent as a man could who is covered in blood and standing over a steroid-pumped freak, also covered in blood.

'Come on, lads, let's go and play football,' I said, walking quickly away, but I'd gone light-headed from blood loss and shock. Besides, the guards could tell it was me who'd beaten Seven Necks just by following the blood trail.

Before the inevitable beating, they frog-marched me to the hospital. I was losing a serious amount of blood and needed stitches. But the nurse there refused to treat me. 'I'm not stitching that man up,' she said. 'Have you seen the man's face he beat? He's in that room there. We've got to get him to hospital. He's in absolute agony.'

I'd almost blinded Seven Necks. I later found out that I'd taken all the jelly out of his head and damaged his corneas. Looking back, it was an appalling outcome to a sickening fight and something I could never imagine doing now, but, at the time, I genuinely didn't care. Some people only understand violence. We'd tried to talk to this bloke, but all he'd done was attack Paul. I'm not proud of that attack, but it had to be done. He'd terrorised too many innocent people and bullied them into submission for too long.

I got a severe bollocking and once again my arse tasted the guards' swords, but, thank God, they didn't add any time to my sentence. And it was worth it. I'd defended Paul, who was the most important person in the world to me, while Seven Necks was a changed man when he came out of hospital three weeks later. He'd got it English style, all right, and he never bullied anybody ever again.

By way of a measure of how much Yare was affecting me, it was only a matter of weeks after the fight with Seven Necks that I had a knife fight with Malacucho, a *Pollo Robo*: the horrible, scarred bastard who'd challenged me to a knife fight on our very first day there.

He'd been winding me up for months, following me around, saying, 'When do we have a proper knife fight, *gringo*?' I'd just shrugged it off. I knew that I wasn't skilled enough in the dark art of fighting with blades. But I also knew that Malacucho would not get off my case until we had our duel, so I set about getting trained for what was to be my first serious knife fight in a Venezuelan jail.

I got Ayala to teach me all he knew. Ayala was an expert knife fighter, widely regarded as the best in all of Yare, as he was the undefeated champion. He'd been in prison for ten years and told me he'd had at least forty knife fights, but there wasn't so much as a mark on him.

Every night, we practised knife fighting in pitch blackness with broom handles set on fire, just like back in La Vega. There was no light at all apart from the burning sticks, training aids that were designed to hurt, but not kill.

At first, I couldn't even get near him. Ayala told me that because I was tall, I had to watch out for my shins. 'Tall men always get stabbed in their legs by smaller men, as they are more agile. They will crack you on the shin with the side of the knife, then stab you in the head when you go down to grab your shin. It's called *rompe coco* – they will crack your coconut open.' The Venezuelan prison knives were perfect for this move as they weren't blades, but big, heavy implements for impaling, which made them perfect for smashing bones, as well as stabbing.

During our sparring, Ayala kept going for my shins, and I completely woke up to that threat. My mentor also told me that tall blokes' long arms meant they were also vulnerable to attacks to their hands, because they put their hands out too far from their bodies, often getting 'cruci-fied like Jesus' through their palms. Not only was that agony, but it meant you had to fight with a dodgy hand.

I'd been warned in La Vega about making sure I didn't go for my opponent's face, and Ayala made the danger in that even clearer to me. 'In Yare, if you stab a guy in the face, his friends will be allowed to shoot you. You will be disgraced by everyone. You will have broken a rule and disrespected him. If it happens by accident, you might just live, but if it is deliberate, well, you have been warned.'

I knew touching another man's face was a big no-no in Venezuelan jails. A couple of months earlier, I'd got into a fight with a con, an ex-copper called *El Tiburon* – 'the shark'. He had touched my face for a joke and, because of the reaction this had provoked in the watching cons around us, we'd had a twenty-minute boxing match that left us both so swollen and bruised, we could barely see. I'd eventually stamped on El Tiburon's leg and stuck my fingers in his eyes, which had caused his friend to pull a gun. 'Leave his face alone, motherfucker. Touch his face again, and I'll kill you.' Talk about double standards.

Ayala's knife training was bruising stuff. I slowly got better, until it got to the point where we were fighting and not touching each other at all.

After fourteen nights of solid training, Ayala turned to me and said, 'You are ready now.'

The next day, when Malacucho once again challenged me to a knife fight, I knew it was time. The fight was set for 8 p.m. that night, in the usual knife fighting area – the back of the gym. People fought there because there were two palm trees that prevented the guards in the watch towers from seeing what was going on.

That evening, I made sure I had got my dirtiest knife on me. This meant that you never cleaned the blade, and dipped them in shit before the fight; it was considered the best treatment for fighting as any cuts then got infected. Disgusting behaviour, but it was just the way the cons did things, and I would have been seen as a soft target if I hadn't done the same.

My final preparation was to follow the advice of numbing my entire face with cocaine. I blasted a few lines up my nose and rubbed it all round my teeth. It heightened my senses to fever pitch and put me right on my toes. Inmates always took cocaine before knife fights as they felt it made them fearless. It was seen as a good fighting aid.

I was shitting it, to be honest. A huge crowd had gathered as word had got round: a knife fight was the most exciting entertainment you got in Yare.

Malacucho was a nasty fighter who really knew his stuff, and I knew I could die. All of his crew were there, all packing guns, as were my mates, who were also fully tooled up with their display guns. It was a clear indication that we would be left to fight it out alone – to the death if necessary. It also meant that the crowd would shoot a man dead if they felt he had broken the rules or disrespected his opponent.

So there we stood, facing each other with our bodies sideways on, our right feet touching – the traditional knife fighting face-off.

Malacucho was scrawny and skinny, but quite long-limbed, like me. Up close, he was one of the ugliest cons I had ever seen. The scar from his mouth up his cheek was like a sick smile, and he had greasy, spiky hair on top with a mullet that kicked up at the back. He was a proper South American shit bag.

I knew that Malacucho knew how to knife fight. Like many of the hardcore *Pollo Robo*s, he had a distinctive fighting style where he stood on the outsides of his feet and rolled from side to side like a bow-legged monkey. These lads never stood flat-footed, as they believed it made them less nimble and easier to hit.

I figured he'd go for my shins, as Ayala had prepped me and, sure enough, he kept lunging that way. But by repeating the same attack, he was predictable. I couldn't get anywhere near his body – he was way too skilful for that – but I realised that each time he went for my legs, he was leaning forward too much and leaving his head exposed.

The next time he steamed in for my shin, I danced back and – *crack*! – I turned my hand over and brought the handle of my heavy iron impaler down on his skull. The sound was like driving a golf ball off the tee, and the whole knife vibrated as if I'd smacked it on a wall. *Rompe coco!* I'd split his coconut.

Malacucho fell to his knees, blood trickling down his face, his eyes fluttering back into his head. I'd beaten him fair and square and, as his crew dragged him away, I felt a sense of elation that justice had finally been done. He'd sought *me* out to pick the fight, not the other way round. Thankfully nobody had died, and our beef was sorted amicably.

Malacucho never bothered me again.

* * *

In jail, you get really attached to your stuff in a way you just don't in civvy street. Good clothes have always been important to me, so I absolutely cherished my Ellesse T-shirt and pumps that had been sent from England. The trouble was, as I'd found out on my very first day in La Vega, decent stuff made you a target for ruthless muggers who would think nothing about sticking a shank in you for a pair of cool shoes.

When we first got to La Vega, I'd 'given away' my Ralph Lauren shirt in exchange for some food and fags (and probably my life). But, three years on, I'd decided I had had enough of bullies trying to take my stuff. Which was why, unbelievably, my *shoes* got me into ugly situations – twice.

BANGED UP ABROAD: HELLHOLE

The first time was with an ugly son of a bitch called Lachuga, over a pair of no-brand trainers.

Most prisoners I came across in Venezuelan jails weren't exactly oil paintings. You'd see every kind of physical deformity known to man there, as well as the usual knife scars, burns, bullet holes, blown-off fingers, hanging-off kneecaps, slashed or missing limbs and chewed-off noses. But, even by their piss-poor standards, this evil-looking guy was one ugly bastard. Lachuga means 'lettuce' and he had earned his nickname because his ears looked like somebody had stuck a lettuce leaf on either side of his head. His ears made a rugby player's look like a supermodel's.

Lettuce was a bit of a joker, and he used to call me Chicken, because he said my white legs and red hair made me look like one. He used to rip the piss out of me constantly, which would have been fair enough, but he was from *el Pollo Robo*, and to be disrespected by one of them stuck in the craw.

Then, one day, I was visited by my girlfriend, Siyanni, the girl I'd met in La Vega. She'd been freed, and would often come to see me. Once again, if we bribed the guards, she was allowed in so we could share a bed.

I'd contacted my dad some weeks earlier, and said that I needed a pair of trainers to play football in, and didn't care what they were so long as they were new. I told him I didn't want any branded trainers, like Nike or Adidas, as they'd just make me a target for a mugging – I like my

The view from our cell in La Vega: two inmates carrying out a drug deal where stabbings frequently occurred.

Two weeks' worth of food: eggs, rice, corn flour, spaghetti, butter and cake mix. That's about £40 of goods – food was more expensive than drugs!

Paul taking a shower. The water was only on for an hour a day, so we had to keep supplies in plastic jugs and ration them.

The La Vega latrine was disgusting. So, we got James' dad to buy some breeze blocks from a local builder and a loo seat, but cockroaches built a nest in the holes.

James getting medical treatment from one of the inmates.
He set fire to the end of a rolled up newspaper to cure trapped
wind. Amazingly, it worked!

The stove we cooked up our business on. Cake and coffee in the
first place, but later we found a more lucrative way to make money.

James passed out inside a La Vega cell. We had 15 knives stashed away behind raunchy posters that the guards were too embarrassed to touch.

James posing with our new mates and holding his first gun. The guy at the front, in the checked trousers, worked for Pablo Escobar and was later killed.

Paul holding the most vital thing you need in a Venezuelan prison – a gun!

Yare in all its glory. The building to the right was where our cells were. Across the patio was The Tower, where anybody who took the metal stairs without permission would get electrocuted.

Through the bars of Yare. That was the warehouse area where we made shoes and the place one guy had his brains blown out in front of us.

The makeshift Christmas tree we drew on to the cell wall to keep our spirits up. This was taken on our third Christmas inside.

With Luis the tattooist, these were our prize fighting knives made from sharpened manhole covers.

Us with our new mates, La Corte Negra gang.

The gang member at the front is holding a homemade shotgun, which we used to patrol our area. These guns were deadly and often went off by mistake or blew up in your hands.

These guys are practising their knife fighting.
One of them was called Popeye because he'd lost
an eye in a real fight and wore a glass replacement.

As you can see Britain was always in our hearts.
Paul painted the Union Jack, his star sign Leo and
the ganga leaves to make us feel at home.

trainers as much as the next man, but I don't want to get a knife in the back for them.

Dad got me some trainers off the market from Leicester. They were by a company called Adore and I'd never heard of the brand. Perfect.

While to an English bloke, they were obviously just a pair of cheap, rip-off trainers, unfortunately, to an uneducated twat like Lettuce, they were worth killing for. They were white and had a Union Jack on them and this Lachuga muppet thought they were Reebok Classics.

On the day in question, I was wearing the new trainers, walking along, minding my own business with my arm around my girlfriend, when Lachuga, who was standing on some stairs next to where we were passing, spotted my trainers and decided he wanted them.

'They're from England,' he said. 'Top-quality shit.' He drew his knife and just lanced off the stairs at me, catching me right across the shoulder with his knife.

The knife went straight in, ripping the muscle off my arm as it went. (I've still got a big scar where the bastard caught me.) I slung Siyanni away, and shouted at her, 'Run! Get out of this fucking prison – right now!' I knew if they took me down, they'd rape her, and maybe even kill her there and then.

With one arm down, I was seriously weakened and open to attack but, thankfully, the scuffle was broken up by some guys I knew and I made off back to my cell. It was first blood to Lachuga.

Back in the cell, I inspected my wound. It was a horrible, deep gash, and I could see all the purple muscle inside. You could even see the knuckle on my shoulder joint, and his knife point had taken a little noggin out of the bone. It was that that really hurt.

With no chance of a visit from a doctor – there was no way on earth the guards would have sent me to hospital, or bothered to call in a doctor for something as petty as a knife wound to the arm – I had to pack salt into my wound to kill any germs. It stung like absolute fuck, but it had to be done, as I was worried he'd got me with a 'dirty' knife. So, I just patched it all up as best I could with some cloth.

For two long months, I kept to my cell and hid away from the world. In the same way lions pick off the weakest gazelles, it would have been suicide to walk the grounds of Yare with a wounded fighting arm.

By now Paul had moved into his own cell. This time gave me space to think. To think about *how* I was thinking. I knew I had changed – life, survival, had come down to the absolute basics, and so had my behaviour. It had to. That was what my knife, my guns, the drug network, were all about. Survival, pure and simple. If I gave that up, or weakened in any way, I was done for. That was what I thought then, and actually, I still think that now. My behaviour might have been basic, brutal, but it kept me – and Paul – alive, I'm sure of that.

Those two months also gave me time to think about Lachuga. I swore vengeance, and dreamed up a thousand ways he would meet his end.

When my arm finally healed, I tracked the guy down in his cell, where he was cooking breakfast. I walked in, unarmed, and threw down the gauntlet.

'Me and you are going to have this out,' I snarled. 'Tomorrow at eight o'clock, we're going to have a knife fight down the back of the gym.'

'What do we have to knife fight for?' he said, acting all innocent, which just wound me up further.

'My trainers,' I said, looking him in the eye. 'You want them? Fine, we will fight for the trainers. If you beat me, they are yours.'

The next night, we headed to the knife fight area. I was pumped up and ready to go, full of cocaine to numb off my head and sharpen my senses.

To make my point, I was going to put my trainers in the middle of the fighting area but, as I was doing so, Lachuga came straight at me with his knife, before we'd even squared off.

The coward lunged forwards to stab me in my guts, but as he came at me, I switched my knife to my other hand – threw it quickly into the other fist, just like I'd been taught – and rammed it hard into his right-hand side, just below his ribs.

As the blade went in, I felt his muscles tighten round it. His flesh clung to my knife like an octopus; it was so fast inside him, I thought maybe I'd gone into a bone. I was tugging at it, trying to get it out, but it was stuck solid.

Lettuce was screaming out in agony, 'No! No! No!', but I just shoved him off. As I did, the blade came free, and I saw a huge spurt of blood shoot out with it, about a metre from his body. Then, another big spurt came out, in time with his heartbeat.

Shocked, all I could think about was that surely Lachuga was beaten. I stood over him and said, 'That's it, lads. He's done,' but as I walked off, he stumbled to his feet and came at me for a second time, trying to take me from behind.

Thank God I saw him, ducked out of the way, and he bundled to the floor, spent. I shouted out, 'That ain't the rules! Fuck off, or I'll do you again!'

All the time, Lachuga was losing a lot of blood. Eventually, he fell to his knees and was rushed off to the hospital.

He'd got what he deserved – and I got to keep my trainers.

It turned out that I'd stabbed Lachuga straight in the liver. We didn't see any more of him after that. Rumour had it he died some time after, and while I'll never know if it was the stab wound that was the beginning of the end for him, I often wonder if that was the case.

Make no mistake, I'm not proud of what I did. In normal circumstances, no one would ever stab a bloke over something as daft as a pair of trainers. But I had had to sort my beef with Lachuga, otherwise every half-arsed bully in the place would have been on to me, and my life would have been gone. Once again, it was do or die.

The second time my footwear got me in hot water was over my favourite pair of Timberland boots. They were my warrior boots. I'd had two knife fights in them and felt very comfortable in them – it was like they brought me good luck. Nobody else liked them; they hadn't heard of the brand, and as they weren't Nike or flash, they just weren't interested.

One day, however, some arsehole took a fancy to them. I'd just finished boxing training for the day, and met Paul, who had been teaching English to some inmates. I had picked up a pair of handmade leather sandals one of my boys had made me, which were a gift for Siyanni, who was due to visit again the next day.

As we walked round a corner, this ponce stuck his homemade shotgun in my face. It was made from an eighteen-inch length of half-inch galvanised pipe, like a mini version of the cow droppers that were stationed on the landings of the Tower.

The prick with the shotgun had wrapped his face in cloth like he was in the Taliban. But he had very distinctive eyes, and I knew exactly who he was. His name was Juan a Dios – John of God (I'd always thought of it as a bit of a gay nickname). Well, God Boy had a mate either side of him, and they were both packing pistols, one a .38 Taurus and the other a snub.

God Boy spat at me, 'We want your boots, and those sandals. Now, motherfucker!'

I thought, 'I've got three guns pointed at me here. That's a twelve-bore with nasty shit in it, and if that laggy [rubber] band goes off, or he slips, I'm dead.' So, I took my Timberlands off, handed them over with Siyanni's shoes and muttered, 'You've got five minutes. Enjoy. Now fuck off, I don't want that wild thing pointing at me.' This was bad. Everybody knew Juan a Dios had just robbed me.

Luckily, the whole scenario had a chilled ending. Paul and I went to see big-man Chico and explained the deal. He issued a directive: 'Return the boots and shoes, today, or the perpetrator will be killed.' Both pairs of shoes came back to me within two hours. That's the power those daddies had.

CHAPTER 7
BAD TIMES

It was around this time that things started to kick off, big time. Tension in the jail was at fever pitch and the root cause of the problem was the whereabouts of the jail's most legendary gun, the Desert Eagle semi-automatic pistol. It had got so bad that gang members were climbing trees and roofs and taking pot-shots at each other. It was like open warfare was going on in the jail.

The Desert Eagle is the same gun Vinnie Jones has in *Snatch*. It's the best pistol money can buy and in Yare, it was the ultimate power. Valued at £1,000 or more, it became the stuff of legend – people had heard its distinctive noise when it went off, and everybody was after it.

By this time the Black Cut had it, but every other gang – and all of the guards – coveted it.

The guards feared the Desert Eagle might spark a riot if anybody tried to take it with force, and had issued a new rule the previous week: nobody was allowed to use firearms to get anything from anybody else. The daddies made it clear that if we wanted something, we had to fight with knives to get it. Finally, guns were off-limits.

But *el Barrio Chinos* decided to ignore that. They really wanted the Desert Eagle – their top men had issued a directive for its capture, and they sent two of their best men, experienced assassins, to go and find it.

These two low lifes toured the prison a few times, and saw a guy with what they thought was the gun. In the ensuing battle, they killed two lads from the Chicken Thieves for it. Ironically, the gun turned out just to be a 9mm Browning – those two boys lost their lives over the wrong gun, and *el Barrio Chinos* had started a war.

The whole prison was immediately put on lockdown. You could cut the atmosphere with a knife. Everybody knew there was a serious, serious storm brewing.

Two hours after this, some idiot decided to open all the locks inside the jail. The National Guard retreated to the gun towers and sat back and watched as the *el Barrio Chinos* were mercilessly slaughtered.

That night, the Black Cut and the Chicken Thieves joined forces and went in and murdered every single *Barrio Chino* they could find on level three of the Tower. It didn't matter if the individual members were involved in the killing of the two boys or not. The whole unit had to die: if you were in the gang, and got caught, you were dead. Full stop.

Over 100 men went onto level three that night and slaughtered everyone they came across. They were chucking grenades in, spraying bullets and setting fire to cells. The gunfire went on for four solid hours.

El Barrio Chinos had built walls of fire on the landings to keep the invaders out, but as these got out of control and the heat got intense, the gang members were running through the flames to try and escape. But they just got cut down by a wall of lead bullets that met them on the other side. Others managed to blow barred windows out and either climbed down three storeys or took their chances and just jumped to escape the raging inferno.

Any that did make it down to the ground then started trying to climb the barbed-wire fences to get away, but they'd only get so far before the National Guard opened fire on them from the gun towers: they'd gone past the yellow line of fire near the prison perimeters.

Meanwhile, we were all lying on the floor of the Annexo, trying to hide. Bullets were flying everywhere going 'Rat-a-tat-a-tat!' for hours. That night, *el Barrio Chinos* were totally wiped out. It was a massacre. All I knew at the time was that this was the most serious shit we'd ever been a part of – what we didn't know was where it was all going to end.

The next day, a very subdued prison population was milling about, when suddenly the prison's main gates burst open. A big military sergeant stormed in clutching a megaphone and started bellowing orders. 'We're coming in, and we're going to clear out any guns we find! We want this Desert Eagle! Resist, and you will die!'

By bad luck, I was nearest to the gate, and a guard came straight at me. He blasted a plastic bullet from his shotgun right into my foot and shouted, 'Move, *gringo*, move!' CS gas canisters were being shot in all directions, and you could barely see through the choking, eye-stinging smog.

Unbelievably, three massive tanks then rolled in through the gate, their gun turrets raised directly at the Tower. Tanks, inside the prison walls? Fair enough, they had to restore order, but these jokers looked like they were invading an enemy state.

Just when we thought it couldn't get any worse, a platoon of soldiers in balaclavas stormed in, armed to the teeth with machine guns and grenades.

Added to this, word had obviously leaked to the outside world about the previous night's violence, because beyond the wire fences we could see vehicles with satellite dishes on top and 'CNN' written down the sides. News crews had gathered, and would film this and show the world.

To stop this happening, however, two of the tanks swivelled their turrets and turned their guns in their direction. It did the trick: the vans fucked off, fast. All we saw were two dust clouds as the reporters belted out of there, gone.

A tense stand-off ensued. Discussions flew around: we knew we had more useful firepower than the army – yeah, they had tanks, but they'd have to flatten the jail, and then come in and get us out. They'd all die trying a siege. The government would never stand for tanks being deployed against prisoners. The tanks were just a threat. Weren't they?

But the blokes in balaclavas were a real worry – were they hiding their identities for a sinister reason? Was there going to be a massacre? Word spread that the prisoners were about to open fire first.

However, high-powered Black Cut bosses calmed the ranks and made the decision to allow the guards in. The guards shredded mattresses and took as many guns as they could find – shit guns that were surrendered, of course, as we couldn't hide all the guns. All the good guns were safely stashed – including the Desert Eagle.

More than sixty men had already died for that gun, and a full-on battle between the army with tanks and 3,000 murderous inmates packing grenades and guns would have been genocide. A war had narrowly been averted.

The guards never did get the Desert Eagle. It was smuggled out of Yare a month later and kept safe until the heat passed.

Later that day, we had to watch as the dead bodies were carried out of the jail. There were four guys to each corpse. It wasn't a nice sight. Some were shot, some blown to pieces, others torched. The whole place had an eerie silence; the only noise was a dog howling.

They used to say in prison, 'When the dog howls, the devil is dancing around.' He'd been dancing, all right. We had seen and heard the whole thing. We'd seen and heard things no man should ever have to go through. It was a waking nightmare, and the worst day of my life.

Unbelievably, too, it was not to be the last massacre we would see within the walls of Yare.

* * *

Even by Yare's shitty standards, I was having a seriously bad day.

It had started out so well. We were meeting Jackie, our contact from the British Embassy. We always looked forward to these times, which happened about once a month or so, as she'd give us updates on our appeal and bring us letters from our families back in the UK. Those letters were a lifeline, and they gave us hope in a world where there was none.

We were especially excited about this particular meeting because we were going to find out how our most recent appeal was getting on. All of our legal updates had to be done via the British Embassy, as the Venezuelan legal system is seriously corrupt at the best of times, and they'd keep you in the dark – or downright lie – at every opportunity. At all of our hearings – where no English had ever been spoken and no interpreter was ever provided – we'd never actually been formally told how long we were to serve in jail. We'd been told verbally by guards that we'd got four years, choosing to believe that the official who had told us our sentence had been increased to ten years at the end of our time in La Vega had been bullshitting.

By this time, we'd served just over three years, so we were really hopeful that that day we might learn of that sacred number in every prisoner's heart: our release date.

With that in mind, we had decided to tell Jackie about the appalling abuses, tortures and beatings that inmates were subjected to inside Yare. We knew the guards were capable of untold savagery. Not only had we seen it happen to others many, many times, but we'd been on the receiving end of their vicious swords several times in the past.

Only days before our meeting with Jackie, the guards had gone too far. They beat us so badly that she reported it – with our agreement – to Amnesty International, and they launched a global awareness campaign against the brutal Venezuelan prison regime.

The night in question, we went by our friend Eddison's cell for a night's session of drinking and smoking.

Eddison was a street robber, a crime which was called '460' because that was the Venezuelan crime number for it. We knew Eddison had also committed murders, but, thankfully, he instantly took to us because he respected the English culture.

We'd give him English lessons and in return he'd lend us salsa CDs, as by now both Paul and I had really got into the local music. It was a real buzz to share cultures. But our latest late-night session had gone on so long, we thought we might risk being late for morning roll call. So we sneaked back across the yard, only to be intercepted by guards. It turned out we weren't anywhere near late, but the guards tried to bribe us anyway, by saying they'd put us down as late if we didn't pay up. We'd refused.

To punish us for this, the guards had made us strip naked and stand against a wall outside. We knew what was coming. Those bastards flayed our arses with their swords in front of 150 inmates who had to stand there, watching, whether they wanted to or not.

The sadistic guards found the whole experience very funny, and had told us to run off if we wanted to avoid any more of this savage beating. I had tried moving but there was blood streaming down my legs, and all the feeling had gone in my legs, so I kept falling down. When we couldn't get away, they'd kicked us for good measure.

At the time, we didn't dare show the hurt to the guards or inmates, and pretended we were all right. But back in my cell, we both wept with the pain. Paul had a huge flap of skin hanging off his lower back, which scarred over, permanently.

He had had enough. This brutality had gone too far.

Paul went to see the governor and showed him his wounds. 'None of my guards did this,' came the reply, although Paul was encouraged to grass on the guard. 'No,' said Paul. 'If I grass him up, my life will not be worth living.'

Paul decided to show Jackie his terrible wounds during our Embassy visit. He told her: 'This is what's going on in here every single day of the week. Every human right going is being totally ignored and crushed. We can't take this shit any more – they'll kill us one day.'

Jackie was absolutely horrified. Nobody had told her about anything like this before. I guess prisoners had been too fearful of even more revenge beatings from the guards, but to Paul's absolute credit he decided to blow the whistle on these bastards.

But in that very same meeting, we were also given some devastating news: 'Guys, you need to steady your-selves for this, because I've got some really bad news for you,' said Jackie. 'The judge has thrown your appeal out of court and they've finalised your sentence. They've increased it again from ten to fifteen years.'

We were absolutely crushed, stunned. 'Why?' we kept asking. 'Why?' It turned out the judge had looked at the amount of drugs we'd originally tried to smuggle – ten kilos of cocaine – and decided that such a large quantity meant he had to throw the book at us, hard.

The irony of it was that every time we'd been to appeal over the years, we'd noticed that the amount of drugs we'd been accused of smuggling had steadily decreased. We were actually arrested for ten kilos, but paperwork said it was seven kilos. In later paperwork it said four kilos. We could only assume that the thieving coppers had steadily skimmed coke off the original stash. We knew that stealing seized drugs to sell for profit was routine, as we'd been told as much by the corrupt prison officials who were the main suppliers of drugs into all the prisons. And, of course, we'd seen those cops sniffing coke off the police van's dashboard outside the hotel. It was unbelievably and staggeringly corrupt. We didn't stand a chance in a system like this. It was absolutely lawless.

While we had expected the cops to tuck into the stash, we did not expect our prison sentence to have been going up and up. We were totally livid this had happened to us, yet powerless, impotent.

We'd served nearly all of our original four-year sentence. We'd gone into that meeting thinking we'd be told a release date. Now, even with exemplary behaviour, there was another two and a half years, at least, that we'd have to serve.

I just lost it. 'Fuck this!' I screamed. 'Fuck this!' And I had to be restrained. I've never been so angry in all my life. I wanted to shoot everybody in that room dead.

To be fair, it wasn't Jackie's fault. We loved her to bits: she did us loads of favours and always gave us hope. She was always great to us under difficult circumstances. She was just the messenger.

I stormed out of the interview room and knew I was capable of anything. I was fed up of the authorities, I was fed up of the corruption and, I suddenly realised, I was fed up of living.

Yare was so dangerous, I'd had to tell my mum not to visit, and that really gnawed at me. I'd also warned Siyanni not to come, either. And there was soon to be another, far more sinister, reason why I didn't want the two most important women in my life anywhere near that hellhole.

After I had got out of the meeting with Jackie, I was told by Black Cut members that word was going around that the Chicken Thieves were saying they were going to gang-rape any women who came into the jail to visit me. They didn't care who they raped: my girlfriend, Embassy officials like Jackie and my mum were mentioned as likely victims for these animals.

When I heard this, it'd be fair to say I went absolutely fucking ballistic. It was time for war. In that moment, I went totally schizo. After everything that had happened – and having just had our hopes of release crushed – I no longer cared if I lived or died.

Until then, I'd always thought first and foremost of my family back home, about serving my time and surviving. Now I just put all of that to the back of my mind. I thought, 'Fuck my family, fuck England, fuck all this, I'm never getting out.'

And that's when I decided to go on a bit of a rampage with a pistol I'd just bought.

I'd bought my bright, shiny Beretta 9mm a couple of weeks before. That day, after all that had happened, I decided that I was going to take it out 'in air', as the saying went.

Out in the exercise yard, I had the gun in my hands, and was walking up to gang members, saying, 'Come on, you cunts! Do you want a taste?' By normal prison rules, I was definitely doing enough to warrant an execution. At any moment, anybody could have shot me dead. Or maybe a bullet through the brain – it would have been easier than the constant mental torture; the constant not knowing what the fuck was going on in your life; the powerlessness of that.

While I was flashing my gun around like a nutter, Paul was keeping well back – he knew there was no reasoning with me then. He filmed me with a video camera we'd had smuggled in (we'd had to leave the last one in La Vega). When I look at that footage now, I see a man who needs help. I was in a different place. I was gone.

I can't explain why no one shot me that day. Perhaps they were so scared by the look in my eyes that day, they backed off. Perhaps they recognised that kind of desperation? Whatever it was, I'd escaped with my life for now.

But, a few days later, I came close to taking it myself.

After the desperate disappointment of the news of having our sentence increased had sent me on my death-wish dance around the prison yard, I vowed to calm down. I didn't want any retribution for losing it with my Beretta.

I started hanging out with Luis and the artier types, and even concentrated on making papier maché vases, which you were allowed to do in the Annexo for a wage. I also cut back on the crack and started smoking more weed to help me chill out.

But, three days later, I was approached by three *Barrio Chinos*. Straight away, I clocked two of them as the lads who had executed the wrong Chicken Thieves for the Desert Eagle pistol. Somehow, they had survived the vicious revenge attack from the Black Cut. But what did they want with me?

Anyway, there they were, as cool as fuck in bandanas. They came up to me and said, 'Hey, *gringo*, we've seen you about, don't you do a lot with the Black Cut?'

I watched them, playing it cool myself. Then one said, 'Your weed smells good; got a smoke?'

'Maybe they hadn't come looking for a beef, after all,' I thought. I was chilled, and let them skin up, but knew this could be a test.

Sure enough, one of them then said, 'Hey, don't you do boxing? Wanna come down the gym with us right now and box?'

My heart raced. The gym was where all the knife fights were held. Days ago, I'd been waving guns in their gang members' faces. I'd done enough to disrespect them and get a knife – or worse – through the head.

I knew these boys were *Barrio* hit men, and I'd been around long enough to know this had all the hallmarks of an impending execution. I thought quickly. Even though I was trying to change my ways, I wasn't so stupid as to go around without a piece. I'd got my Beretta in my shorts, and as I didn't want to lose face, I agreed to go with them for a box.

When we got to the gym, one of the gangsters said, 'Hey, let me look at your gun, *amigo*. Let me hold it for you.' He went to grab it, but I stopped him.

'Lay off, it's not on the safety catch,' I said. 'I never have it on the safety.'

'Neither is mine,' he said, and pulled out a .38 snub, a lovely, chrome seven-shooter, and started whirring the chamber round.

I decided the best thing to do was to front him out and said, 'There ain't no bullets in that.'

'Sure there is, *hombre*; it's all loaded up,' he grinned, and showed me there were bullets in all seven chambers of his gun.

I knew I had to take control of the situation. We all had shooters, but there were three of them and pulling mine would have meant certain death. But I found that I was still so pissed off with life, I didn't care.

I just wanted to make sure that if I was to die, I'd take some of these twats with me.

I knew these *Barrio* guys were young, immature and easy to manipulate if you challenged their manhood, so

I said, 'Hey, have you guys ever played Russian roulette? It's a game where you have one bullet in the chamber, spin it, put the gun in your mouth and fire it.'

I'd played Russian roulette a few times before in Yare. It had been the punishment for losing at Ludo, to spice things up a bit in the evenings, and we'd reversed the ratio: with only a one in six chance of the gun going off, nobody had ever been hurt.

When I put *el Barrio Chinos* on the spot like that, and challenged them, they all went quiet and inquisitive.

'You normally play with only one bullet,' I said, 'so you've got to take at least two bullets out of this gun to make it fair.'

The guy holding the gun took two bullets out of his snub. That meant there were still five bullets left. The odds were stacked against us.

He looked around and saw a guy who was flaked out on the canvas, as he'd just finished a sparring session in the boxing ring. He walked up to him, pointed the gun straight at his head and pulled the trigger.

Click!

The *Chino* shouted at me, 'Is that how you do it?', as the guy cowered on the floor, nearly having a heart attack with terror. He'd just been sitting there minding his own business.

Now it was my turn.

There was no escaping it. I had to go next. If I didn't, they'd probably kill me anyway. I said, 'Come over here, you mad head, and give me the fucking gun.'

With the .38 snub in my right hand, I placed my left hand on the chamber, looked the *Chino* straight in the eye and spun the chamber. It whirled for a couple of seconds, then stopped. I tensed myself, placed the barrel in my mouth and …

Click!

The hammer flicked down and nothing happened. I'd got away with it! I'd had a five in seven chance of certain death and lived to tell the tale. It was the scariest, most reckless thing I'd ever done. I can still taste the metal of the barrel. I can still taste the gunpowder residue off the bullet shot before.

But the next guy wasn't so lucky.

Click, *bang!*

The bullet went down through his neck and blew all the back of his neck out, all over the wall. There was blood everywhere and even now I still see his eyes flickering as he went. I can still see the moment he died in front of me. His last breath. It spooked me out quite a bit. I mean, he could have been someone's dad, or someone's son.

Afterwards, Paul was really upset with me. He said to me, 'What are you doing? What am I going to do if you're not here? I'd never make it on my own.' But I had no more need to go on with life. I wanted to end it.

To make matters worse, soon after this, getting Amnesty International involved over the beating me and Paul took from the guards came back to haunt us.

Both the governor of the prison and the Embassy had kept pestering Paul to point out which guard had beaten us. It wasn't in Paul's nature to grass, but this bastard had still been dishing out kickings to other cons – he was a born sadist. Finally, when the governor had asked Paul about it for the umpteenth time, he had just walked out, pointed in the twat's face and said, 'It was him.'

The guard had rasped, '*Sapo!*' – 'grass' – but he had got what was coming to him and was sacked.

We then heard that the other guard who'd beaten our arses with his sword was going to get the sack, too. Worse for him, we heard he could also end up in jail. And there's nothing worse than being an ex-copper in a Venezuelan jail. Those guys get it worse than the sex offenders.

It also meant that Paul and I had made some bad enemies.

One evening, I was sitting in my cell on my own when this guard walked up to my door. It was, thank God, locked.

He had on a black Bob Marley T-shirt, with black combat bottoms, and had obviously just come off his shift. Suddenly, he rammed his shotgun through the bars, right into my face.

'You fucking *gringo* pig, if you get me the fucking sack I'll have you blown up!' he shouted.

I couldn't let the guy talk to me like that. Not in front of everyone, and particularly not after what he'd done to us.

'Listen, mate, calm down, get that fucking gun out of my face and just remember where the fuck you are,' I replied. 'Back off, or I'll stick a bullet in your head tomorrow.' I had to face him down.

'You fucking what?' he screamed back at me. 'You cannot do that to me in my own country!' he raged.

'This is my country, too, now,' I told him. 'I've been in here a long time and this is my house. Threaten me in my own house, and I will kill you.' I sneered at him and went on: 'Your poxy shotgun with plastic bullets? You have to be within twenty yards to hit me. But with my guns, I can shoot you from anywhere.' I gestured round the cell block. 'Any of these little holes in these walls, I can shoot from. Don't you forget that. I can shoot you any time, from anywhere. You can't go using your gun round here. But I can. And there are 300 mates of mine in here who will shoot you, too. They'd be more than willing. So take that fucking gun out of my face or you will die.'

'But you will get me the sack – I could go to prison!' he said, more pleading now than threatening.

'You should have thought about that before you went and beat the shit out of us,' I said. 'So get that fucking gun out of my face, NOW!'

He'd basically lost it. In his anger, he'd broken one of the unwritten rules of Yare. He'd brought his battle into my house. He went home to his family every night, but that cell, that was my house. Now, I had the right to attack him.

But we never saw him again. Maybe he did get the sack, maybe they just transferred him to another jail. Who knows? The bastard was gone. And it was best for both of us. Because, after that night, if he hadn't killed me first, I swear I'd have had to kill him, or got somebody else to do it for me.

Kill or be killed.

The Amnesty International campaign did have one upside, however, though not from the quarter we'd expected to receive advantage.

Representatives from twenty-four countries, from Canada to Australia to Hong Kong, wrote to us, giving us their support. They'd also written to my mum and dad in England, offering their condolences for what we'd been put through.

When we saw this great big wad of letters, about three inches thick in total, we thought, 'Hey up, something might come of this.' Some of those letters were five pages long, and they promised to look into things for us.

But it would appear that none of them actually did anything. Nobody came to visit us to get our full story or speak to us – they just paid lip service, and sod all happened.

Nothing concrete ever came of the whole palaver, except for one thing: by getting that bastard booted, it got us respect from the other prisoners. Nobody had ever stood up to those shits like that before, and we were foreigners, so it resonated even more with the local lads.

It gave us kudos, which was vital in taking heat away from us a while. Respect buys you breathing space, and Paul played a blinder in that respect. And it made the guards think twice about hoofing us in the future.

* * *

After my game of Russian roulette had ended with the death of a *Barrio Chino*, I finally became aware of Theo, who was the big boss of the gang.

I'd heard about this bad ass before as Eddison had told me he was a proper bad boy. Even though he was only nineteen, Theo had huge power. He was in for high-degree murders, and specialised in robbing the rich and murdering their bodyguards. He'd work with a partner who rode a motorbike, with Theo on the back; they'd steam into their victims, all guns blazing. In Venezuela, robbery is a very different game. Because it's legal for anybody to carry a gun, you have to assume the guy you're mugging will be armed, so it's shoot first, and rob the corpse.

I also knew Theo had shot a lot of gang members in lots of different jails and, as a result, he had a heavy death sentence on his head as so many cons wanted him dead. But he had money and power, and wasn't a dickhead. He'd even intimidated one of the guards into making sure Theo got all the armour he needed into jail directly from the streets, with no stupid mark-up on the price.

One day, we were sitting around smoking, when this very scary-looking half-Chinese, half-Venezuelan dude walked into my cell and plonked himself down next to me.

'Hey, motherfucker, you like to smoke? Here, try some of this shit,' he said, and he handed me a bag of weed. 'My name is Theo. I'm the head of *el Barrio Chinos*.'

'Nice to meet you, I'm Jim,' I said, and shook his hand. 'I met a few of your boys the other day; we had a little game together.'

'Yeah, I heard about that.' The cell fell silent. One of his boys had blown his head off because of me. Had he come round for revenge? Was it time for an eye for an eye? But instead, he asked, 'Is it time for you to join us in *el Barrio Chinos*?'

To say my arse cheeks were flapping would be an understatement. He could have sliced my throat on the spot for what I'd done, but instead he was asking me if I wanted to join his gang.

I waited a beat, then replied, 'I'm flattered, but you know I run with the Black Cuts. If I dropped them for you, you know my life would not be worth living.'

'OK,' he said. 'We talk with them. We all get on so long as nobody fucks with our programme. I just wanted to know that you're with me. Because a lot of people in Yare, they want me dead.' He looked at me. 'I'm pissed off with it, *hombre*. My girl visits me tomorrow, and I haven't seen her in two years. I don't want her to come, she might get killed.' He sighed. 'I can't even walk around here without some prick trying to bump me off. My boys, they sorted some guy out last week – he won't be bothering me any time soon – but other motherfuckers that run with him, his brothers and cousins, will come in from other jails and come after me. Then, we will have to deal with them.'

He went on to tell us how his rep was such that he couldn't even carry a gun, he was searched so often. But then he pulled down his Mickey Mouse sock and showed us a little Colt Derringer, a double-barrelled ball-bearing gun he had stashed. It looked classic, an antique, but a bit feeble with its two pull-back hammers.

'What good will that little thing do?' I asked, daringly.

'It will blow your fucking head off, *amigo*,' he said. 'It's a baby shotgun. *Boom, boom*.' He mimed shooting me in the head. 'And this is my sniper gun,' he said, pulling out a .22 pistol from his other sock. It looked like a cowboy gun, and had a beautiful ivory handle. The .22 bullets had been turned into dum-dums, so while small, they would blow great holes through a man.

'I'm showing you my pieces because I want word spread: anybody who fucks with me when my girl's here, they will wind up dead. *Comprendez?*' And with that, he walked out.

About a week later, we heard that two coppers had walked into his cell on level three of the Tower. Each cell was separated by sheets, pulled tight on cords and nailed to the floor. The rule was clear: if you touched somebody else's sheet, you'd get stabbed or shot. In particular, when you had a girl over for a conjugal visit, your cell was sacred, even if your neighbours could hear you screwing her through the sheet.

Anyway, the two cops had walked in on Theo when his bird was on top of him. He'd gone fucking mad, but they'd just told him to calm down and shut up.

Later that night, those two cops had gone up to do a name check, but they hadn't come back down. All that night, we could hear noisy, grating sounds coming from across the yard. The rumour was that Theo had had the two guards executed, then chopped them into little pieces with machetes. The grating was the sound of stones being used on the blades to keep them sharp. Apparently, they had chopped them up so they could dispose of the body parts more easily – they threw these down into the moat that ran all round the Tower, about twelve feet away from the walls.

I believed the story – for days after, there was a horrible stink coming from the moat as the guards' remains rotted away in the heat.

While it was all very flattering to be approached by Theo, the National Guards were getting very heavy with me. They couldn't get near *el Corte Negra* or *el Barrio Chinos*, but because I was friends with both, I think they saw me as a threat.

A favourite trick of theirs was to blatantly throw drugs in front of me, then accuse me of dropping them just so they could give me a good kicking, thrash me with their sticks or smash my arse with their swords.

One particular time, this practice nearly got me in big trouble. I was walking along, minding my own business, when a guard threw a bag of weed down near me, and said: '*Gringo*, you lost something, now get against the wall!'

At the time, I'd decided to follow a god called Caravaca – the god of mischief – mainly because the Black Cut did, but also because the prison allowed you to wear the special crucifix the cult had around your neck on a length of rope. As it happened, also attached to this rope, under my T-shirt, was my knife.

You had to carry a knife at all times, but you'd get a severe beating if a National Guard caught you with one. So, with this guard frisking me down after a bogus drug plant, I was about to be severely stitched up. Thinking quickly, I leaned forward as far as I could, which meant the heavy knife swung away from my body. As the guard searched me close to my body, he totally missed the impaler. Caravaca was certainly looking after me that day.

Even better, a mate of mine saw the bag of weed and snatched it during my frisk, and we smoked it later. A small victory over the guards, maybe, but a good one.

CHAPTER 8
NO MERCY

You might think I'm exaggerating when I say that corruption runs and has always run to the very top of the tree in Venezuela, but it's true. Hugo Chavez, the current president of Venezuela, has even served time in Yare prison, trying to fight it.

Back in the 1990s, Chavez had been a military officer who'd started his own revolutionary political party to try and overthrow the horribly corrupt government of the time. For his troubles, he was banged up in Yare for two years after leading a military coup to topple the former president in 1992.

Upon his release from Yare, Chavez mobilised an army and drove to the Venezuelan ministerial palace with tanks, which eventually led to him being elected President Hugo Chavez in 1999.

Despite numerous charges of human rights abuses and corruption himself, Chavez is worshipped by millions of ordinary Venezuelans for bringing a democracy of sorts to their nation, and they especially love the way he has always stood up to the USA. Truly, I believe Venezuela could take on America, not because they have a military arsenal equal to America's, but because every single man, woman and child would be prepared to fight and die for Chavez in the streets.

I've got a lot of respect for the guy, and he was particularly loved by the prison population. They saw him as one of their own. His legendary status was only increased when he decided to bring in a new law that pardoned all prisoners who had served more than two years in jail. Having served two years himself, he said that it was his experience that convicts had learned their lesson after that time, and keeping them inside for longer was just cruel.

The new law came into effect while we were in Yare, and many long-term cons walked free. But for some reason – best known only to the jail's governors – they decided not to bring the law in to Yare.

As you can imagine, this went down like a shit sandwich with Yare's inmates.

As a result, several of the prison's high-powered inmates began lobbying the jail's governor, trying to force him to get some of the country's top judges to visit the jail and look at their paperwork, hoping they'd set them free. It might sound odd that judges came to visit the cons rather than the other way around, but it was deemed too risky to allow these kind of men out of the prison's four walls. They had too many accomplices on the outside, ready and willing to hijack prison vans.

But to really get the message across, it was initially decided that the prison should go on a mass hunger strike. It wasn't optional: it was made clear to us that everyone in Yare had to obey this 3,000-man fast. If you were caught with any food at any time, you would be stabbed or tortured for it. We didn't have any choice in the matter.

I defy anybody to say no to psychopaths like those. If we'd been found eating, we'd have been carved up and thrown in the Tower moat before we'd even had chance to digest. As incentives to skip a meal goes, it certainly beat Weight Watchers.

But, it was decided, that wasn't enough. To make a gruesome point to the prison's bosses, it was decided that every inmate should have their mouths sewn up with three stitches of cotton through our lips to keep us from opening our mouths more than a crack.

Paul had to sew my mouth up and I did his. We numbed our mouths with ice beforehand and had a few shots of rum, then just did it. But it still hurt like hell.

All we were allowed, to stop us from dying of dehydration, were cups of sugared water that we had to suck through the gap at the side of our mouths. It was just enough to keep us going.

*

After a few days of this we were all starting to hallucinate. We felt so lethargic. Another drawback was that as we were too weak to do anything, we started thinking too much about the situation we were in. It totally did my head in. Time is the number one enemy of the long-term inmate, and the hunger strike just made the days pass in slow motion. Every second felt like an hour.

Everybody kept saying it was going to be over soon, but I was getting severely agitated by it all. But I ground it out, and stuck at it. Apart from the immediate fear of torture, those that didn't would never have been able to live down the shame. They'd have been an outcast forever.

The worst thing was that, during visits, girlfriends and family brought food parcels. It was one of the highlights of any inmate's time there, and really something to look forward to. I told Siyanni it was safe enough for a visit but that I couldn't accept any gifts from her when she came. I couldn't bear the temptation of biscuits and cakes sitting in my room when I knew that the punishment would be a cold, steel blade between the ribs.

We didn't have scales to weigh ourselves with, but I lost no end of weight, and I didn't feel good at all.

The strike went on for eight agonising days, when suddenly word went round that the hunger strike was over. Our happiness lasted for about ten seconds, then we realised we would have to take the three stitches out of our lips. These had by now scabbed over, gluing the cotton to our flesh. Once again, Paul and I numbed the area with ice, hit the rum and carefully snipped each other's lips free.

Naturally, with that grim DIY surgery out of the way, the first thing our minds turned to was food – any old food. The trouble was, there was nothing in the jail until the next prison visit, which was in two days' time. The prison was totally bare, apart from our basic rations of rice and salt. We had two carrier bags of rice and a pouch of salt to share between eighteen lads, which was never going to go round. Jesus might have been able to feed 5,000 with a few loaves of bread and some fish, but let me assure you that two bags of rice will not feed eighteen murderers, drug smugglers and bank robbers on a normal day, never mind when they've been on hunger strike for more than a week.

When you've eaten bugger all for over a week, two more days seem like a life sentence away. So, we frantically scrabbled around looking for something – anything – to eat.

In desperation, we decided to cook up a big *sambumbi* – the huge South American rice dish where you chuck in any old stuff you can get your hungry hands on – spaghetti, meat, whatever – into the concoction, then fry it all up. But what meat could we possibly find to eat?

And that's when our hungry eyes fell on Chiquita the cat.

Chiquita belonged to Eddison, and prowled his warehouse looking for rats to kill. In Yare, prisoners were allowed pets, as long as they fed them. Many inmates kept dogs as companions, and would often set them on enemies to dole out a mauling. More than one time, I saw a con stab a dog that had been set on him. It was horrid.

'Right,' we said to Eddison, 'we've decided. We've taken a vote and we're going to eat Chiquita.'

He went berserk. 'Motherfuckers, you cannot kill my cat! She keeps the rats down in the warehouse. That bitch pays her way. Kill her over my dead body!'

We could see we were getting nowhere, so I decided to change tack. 'Rats, you say? Where do the rats live?'

'There's a rats' nest up in the roof at the back, where Chiquita always hangs out. There are hundreds of the bastards. Fuck off and catch a rat if you want some meat, *hombre.*'

No prizes for guessing what was going through my mind: fried rat for dinner suddenly didn't seem so bad. By this point, I was so hungry, I'd have considered chopping my own arm off and sticking it in a baguette.

So, we took Chiquita up onto the warehouse roof and, sure enough, there was a huge, tangled rats' nest up there, inside a stinking pile of twigs, rags, old plastic bottles and assorted other garbage. We sent Chiquita in and, seconds later, there was a furious scrabbling and high-pitched squeal, and she came out with a nice, fat rat in her mouth. It was about fourteen inches long nose to tail-tip, still alive and squawking as Chiquita played with it.

We took it downstairs, and feverishly chopped off its head, claws and tail, then gutted it. But then Paul said, 'I bet that fucking thing's full of disease,' and our gnawing appetites wavered.

'No, we'll make it good,' I said, and proceeded to shave the still-warm rat's fur off with a Bic razor, then, for good measure, washed its skin with a big block of blue prison soap that stank like bog cleaner.

We boiled it for a bit, took it out, sliced it, diced it, lobbed it in the rice and fried it up. We were doing that shit years before *I'm A Celebrity Get Me Out Of Here!* It was quite all right, as it goes – a bit bacon-y, and we put in so much salt, you could barely taste it, anyway. We had one rat between eighteen lads, but we all got a couple of decent chunks.

As we cooked it, Paul and I were laughing at what we were doing, and saying that all the lads back in England would never believe what we had come to – that we had to eat vermin to stay alive.

Chiquita, too, lived to see another day, and kept kicking out kittens, which, to this day, probably keep Yare's inmates in fried rat, if they ever get desperate enough.

Even though 3,000 men had been through the hell of an eight-day hunger strike, the governor, in his wisdom, did jack about it. So the enraged gangster bosses decided to take fierce and direct action.

The first we knew about it was when they marched the governor into the main yard, wearing only his underpants, and demanded that he tell the assembled masses why he was choosing to ignore their – and the president's – wishes.

When he refused, the daddies told him, 'You get the judges down here, or we're going to start sending bodies out every fucking day. Five men will die every single day, and you will have their blood on your hands.'

When the governor said he couldn't do that, somebody shot at him.

Being fired at scared him so much, he shat his pants. You could see he'd messed himself when he turned and ran off back to his quarters.

We started laughing our heads off at this, but slowly stopped when we realised we were going to get fucked over again, as the governor would now have to send a militia in to take all the guns in the prison back again.

Once again, the future of Yare was balanced on a tense knife edge.

The very next day, hundreds of guards came in at dawn, and they took every bit of metal that wasn't bolted down or hidden. Of course, we'd stashed most of our decent shooters, fearing the obvious threat of an armed raid.

A lot of armoury was still seized, however, and tension in the jail just got worse. Both sides were backed into a corner, and neither was prepared to give way.

Two days later, true to their word, the gang leaders hand-picked men from a list the daddies wanted bumped off and started killing them, sending their bodies out. All hell broke loose.

I was playing football when a salvo of gunfire broke out between the Tower and the guards' quarters. To my left, I could see a tree being shredded as bullets flew through the branches. This was kicking off, big style.

I started running for my life when I felt a bullet rip past my chest. I looked down and I was covered in blood. I'd been hit.

I scrambled back towards my block, but the way was blocked by a guard, who shouted, 'Where the fuck are you going?', and shot me in the chest with a canister of tear gas. It knocked the wind out of me, but I kept on running for the cover of my cell block. Then another guard suddenly appeared and blasted my foot with a plastic bullet from point-blank range, melting my trainer to my foot.

By the time I got back, my white T-shirt was covered in blood. I lifted it up and said to Paul, 'Have I been hit?'

Luckily the bullet in the yard had just skimmed me and burned my skin. 'It's just skimmed you, kid!' Paul kept saying, reassuring himself as much as me, I think. We kept ourselves busy, spending ages picking bits of plastic out of my foot with tweezers.

A full-on gun battle followed between the guards and the Tower. You could see bullets tearing into the walls, with puffs of dust everywhere. They were out to kill people that night – the National Guard wanted us dead.

A little while after this, the guards came into our cell block and said, 'We're doing a search, get the fuck outside, now!' They started smashing all our stuff – they got my TV, radio, aftershave and everything else I owned, and made us all go and sit on the ground outside, in front of the Tower.

I knew our lives were in danger. It was madness to sit outside the Tower at the best of times, never mind in the middle of a gunfight. I said to Paul, 'I'm telling you, they're going to open fire on us and the guards. You watch, we're fucking dead!'

Sure enough, all of a sudden the legs of a guy sitting three people away from me flew into the air as he fell back, shot in the groin. The guns were ripping off again – all I could see was mud skimming up where bullets were tearing into the ground around us. We were sitting ducks.

I ran and dived into one of the inspection pits where the vehicles were searched on the way into the jail. Everybody pissed and shat into these holes, but I didn't care. I quickly made the decision that I'd rather swim in shit than drown in my own blood any day, and at least nobody could shoot at us there.

The guards were screaming at us to come out, but we knew their plastic bullets couldn't kill us, so we took our chances and stayed put. But the sods fired tear gas in, and we were forced back out into the open.

I took my chances and sprinted back to my cell block, making it through the door and diving for cover on the floor.

The guards were still in there searching our cells, and I shouted, 'You did that on fucking purpose! You put us out in the line of fire!'

One guard turned to me and said, calm as you like, 'Sure. The numbers have got to go down. If your own inmates are killing you anyway, what does it matter if we use you as bait?'

I could not believe those arseholes were saying this. They'd lined up about sixty of us and made us target practice for the psychos in the Tower. They'd put all of us there to get shot, for the specific reason they wanted us dead and gone.

The lad who was shot in the groin later died of blood loss. They didn't care. To them, we were no more than sub-human. All I can say now is, it's no wonder that when you treat people like animals for long enough, they start to bite back.

After all the bloodshed, word finally got out and one of the country's top judges visited Yare to look at inmates' paperwork with a view to granting some of Chavez's presidential pardons. One of the most vicious psychopaths in the whole joint, and his sidekick who'd killed four men only the week before, were granted a release.

They had been doing time for murder, but we were kept in for moving cocaine. I admit that in some people's eyes we could have been committing murder, too, by helping get drugs onto Britain's streets. But that would be through the drug taker's choice.

It summed up the entire rotten Venezuelan justice system for me. You could get twenty-five years for getting caught with a bag of puff in this country, but blokes who'd murdered three or four people could be out in seven months if they admitted their crime. When we asked the guards about it, they said they preferred it if murderers admitted their wrongs, as they could throw them in jail to teach them a lesson, then let them go, without having to send them repeatedly to court for appeals and deal with all the resulting paperwork. So, murderers walked free early, simply because some copper couldn't be arsed to fill out a couple of forms. Truly, you couldn't make it up.

* * *

During all my time in Yare, I thankfully never needed to shoot at anybody with one of my own guns. But I did shoot to kill with a gun I'd borrowed off a mate. And I was trying to kill a man over a £2.50 debt.

The guy I tried to kill was one of the lowest forms of prison life. Nicknamed *el Brujas* – which translates as 'grassing witches' – these were pond-life inmates who smoked crack, and cleaned the guards' toilets and rooms for pin money.

You couldn't trust them as far as you could throw them. They would steal your dying breath if they could sell it for crack money. Crack addiction could suck out a man's soul like a vampire, leaving only an empty husk behind if you let it. They were so hated, they weren't allowed in the units with the regular prisoners, and were so low, they'd even gone beyond the point of being worth being marked, stabbed or raped for vengeance. They didn't even have knives or guns. If they were caught stealing, the usual punishment was to whack a belt around their legs, another around their arms, then throw them onto a bed and whack a deodorant up their arse. I'm talking about one of the glass, roll-on deodorant bottles. I'd seen many of the bastards be held down as someone put the deodorant near their arsehole, then palm it, whack, straight up.

It sounds sadistic, but those fucking addicts were so low, it was the only way of getting through to them.

A lot of them were kids with rich parents, and they all had a similar story to tell. They'd just gone down the wrong path. They didn't know about violence, and had no real way of defending themselves. They'd rebelled against their mums and dads and wound up as crack addicts, and their poor parents had no choice in the end but to throw them out on the streets.

It must have been tough for those kids, but you still had to be careful with them, because when they needed crack, they'd pull a knife on you happily and stab you up for their next fix. They became like killer, crack-crazed zombies.

And if they couldn't beg or steal drugs, they'd go to even more horrible lengths to get their next fix. Paul and I had watched in transfixed horror one time when a user who had some crack told another man he'd let him have a rock if he performed oral sex on him.

The guy had agreed.

We'd thought he was joking, but when he had nodded yes with wild eyes, the other man had unzipped his flies and placed a small rock of crack on the tip of his erect penis, saying, 'You want it, bitch? You know what to do …'

To our horror, the addict had gone down on him and done the business.

The desperate lengths crack addicts would go to came back to haunt me as I shot at someone over the £2.50 debt.

But then the guy, Sanchez, had tried to hack my arm off with a machete.

I'd given him £2 to run and get me some weed, and I'd even given him an extra 50p to score a stone of crack for himself, because I'm nice like that and thought it would mean he wouldn't double-cross me.

I was gagging for a smoke, and I knew I wouldn't sleep until I'd had one. I was pacing up and down, rest-lessly, but after four hours Sanchez still wasn't back and I decided to go looking for him in the neighbouring jail block, which was where you went to score your puff at night.

To get to there, I had to go across the exercise area, and it was common knowledge that anybody who went out there after dark was fair game to be murdered – by both inmates and screws alike. But I was so pissed off by this time that I just didn't care. I was convinced that Sanchez had robbed me blind and he was going to pay.

I set off, weaving in and out of all the buildings, hoping that none of the guards could see me or, if they could, that they wouldn't get a clear shot at me.

Above the gate to the building was a big box full of guards, so I hid in a bush and started calling out, 'Over here! Over here!' I knew those guys could be bribed, and would even sell you drugs if you caught the right one. Sure enough, a guard came over, and I scored a £2 bag of weed off him.

'Have you seen Sanchez?' I asked.

'No, *amigo*, he hasn't been over here. Try over by the dining hall, that's where all those scum do their crack.'

I was making my way there when, suddenly, the silence was ripped apart. 'Bam bam!' – one of the guards in the gun turret had shot two bullets at me. Dust flew up around me as the bullets tore into the ground, and I heard the guard cocking his gun again, ready to spray off some more lead in my direction.

I just thought, 'Fuck this, see you later,' and instinctively tore off back towards the Annexo, once again weaving between the buildings, jumping into the shadows and wriggling through bushes.

Safely out of range, however, I changed my mind and made my way back towards the dining hall. I wanted to see this bastard. Sure enough, there was Sanchez, kneeling down and firing up his lighter, taking a hit of crack I'd paid for.

I'd got my gun on me, and reached for it. I was determined to shoot him – just pop one in his leg to teach him. But letting off my gun out there would have been suicide, given the amount of guards around.

So I had to wait. Back at my cell, I told the lads Sanchez was going to get it. I was furious, going on about how he'd robbed my money for crack, totally taken the piss and violated my trust.

The fact that I was preparing to take a man's life for £2.50 didn't occur to me at the time. It was a matter of principle – prison principle.

About a week later, I was on the fifth floor of the Annexo looking down at the garden area, when I saw Sanchez milling about down there. He did a bit of gardening for the cops to earn money, and he'd got a big machete in his hand where he'd been chopping down weeds. His mate was also walking along with a shovel on his back, so I knew they were both tooled up.

I thought about dashing back to my cell to get my gun or knife, but it would have taken too long. Once again, I decided to sort this one English-style.

I ran down five flights of stairs in record time, and timed it perfectly so that Sanchez was just coming past the Annexo entrance when I flew at him and volleyed him with a right hand, whack, straight across the jaw.

The little piece of shit span round and hit the deck, and I went to jump on him, but his mate came at me with the shovel and, in the kerfuffle, Sanchez sprinted off.

By this time, a big commotion had broken out and I knew I was being watched. It was far wiser to stick it to a bloke on the quiet, or in an organised fight, as doing the business in full view of the guards always meant a severe pasting. Once again, I had to bide my time.

Two days later, however, I was in the dinner queue with Paul when I saw a flash of silver out of the corner of my eye. I put up my arm instinctively, just in time, as Sanchez's machete was mid-swing, slashing down at me. I felt the tip of the blade whizz past my arm, cutting the skin but thankfully not causing any real damage.

Unbelievably, Sanchez had tried to hack my arm off my body. And in the canteen, of all places.

The guards went apeshit, and put the whole place on lockdown.

Now that the entire prison knew about my beef with Sanchez, and I'd lost face, I knew I had no choice but to deal with this problem fully, once and for all.

I started to hang around on level five of the Tower with the Black Cut, sitting there with my Beretta 9mm, biding my time, waiting for Sanchez to appear in the yard below. I knew I was going to shoot him dead. I'd become so consumed by the ways of Yare, I was ready to kill him over a poxy £2.50 drug debt.

A couple of days later, Sanchez appeared below, walking through a hole in the chicken wire fence that surrounded the gardens. I let him come through, loading my gun as I watched him do a drug deal with his mate. Then I coolly took aim and – 'Bam bam!' – let off two shots.

I saw a shower of blood erupt from his neck, he went down and his body was jerking on the ground. I'd got the little bastard.

But the Black Cut were furious I'd carried out my attack from their territory, fearing a huge search and grim physical retribution from the officials who'd try everything in their power to extract the name of the attacker and the weapon from level five. They quickly began stashing everything – guns, drugs, weapons – and, sure enough, there were suddenly swarms of severely pissed-off guards everywhere, hollering at us and pumping their shotguns back, ready to fire at will.

Thinking quickly, I just said, 'Don't worry about it, lads. I'll sort it.' And so, when the livid guards asked who had carried out the attack, I stepped up and said, 'It was me. I did it.'

This was unheard of. Nobody in their right mind ever admitted to a gun attack: the torture and beatings that followed meant inmates usually chose to lie low and hope they got away with it.

But I'd brought trouble right to the door of the Black Cut. If the guards performed a serious shakedown of level five, they'd seize as many weapons as possible, leaving the Black Cut open to possible attack and annihilation by other gangs. Admitting to my crime to the guards was going to be painful. But it would be a lot less painful than crossing the Black Cut.

'Which fucking gun did you use?' they bellowed, and I fished out a knackered old .38 that looked like something out of an old Clint Eastwood movie. It was a piece of shit that wouldn't be missed. They grabbed the gun off me, shoved me against a wall and made me drop my shorts.

As the whole level looked on in grim silence, the head guard stepped up, drew his dreaded sword and gave me eight smashes across my bare arse with the flat of the blade. It was agony. Blood was streaming down my legs, the skin hanging off my buttocks.

Nobody saw Sanchez for three months and we all thought he was dead. Then, one day, the lads came in and told me Sanchez was alive. He was in a wheelchair, crippled. Slobbering and everything. Turns out a bullet had gone straight through his spine and had paralysed him.

I saw him one day in the canteen. He was being pushed by his friend, who looked at me right in the eye, and shook his head.

After the initial shock, I felt awful. What had become of me? I reasoned, Sanchez had tried to hack my arm off in the canteen. He could have killed me right there. Basically, our beef wouldn't have gone away until one of us was dead – that was the law in Venezuelan jails: it really was kill or be killed. But the sight had sickened me. I'm not happy about what I did to Sanchez, but I'm alive to tell the tale. I have to focus on that, or I'd go mad with the guilt. It was the behaviour of the person Yare had made me become, and not *me*. But it will live with me forever. I was so mentally unstable back then.

In Yare, we saw the most horrific acts of violence and cruelty we'd ever witnessed carried out man against man. Worse, I knew all of the horrific shit I was witnessing was turning me into a different person. But the very worst was yet to come.

A new boy, a half-Brazilian kid called Joseph, came into the jail, and right from the off acted like a total jack the lad. He told everybody he was a solo bank robber, but this was very unlikely as they always operated as part of a gang, so senior gang members bribed the secretaries to see this guy's file.

This was a routine practice. Gang members made it their top priority to find out who was coming into their unit as it could be a matter of life or death if they were related to or ran with somebody they'd got a beef with. We'd been checked out this way ourselves when we'd turned up. Before we even got there, the gang bosses knew we were in for drugs offences, so they didn't need to worry about us trying to take them out.

Senior gang members would often approach new boys and ask them, 'What do you want? Peace? Or violence? Or bullshit?', but with Joseph, they decided to test him by getting him to bump off troublesome inmates they wanted dead.

Within weeks, he'd stabbed or shot about fifteen men dead. Joseph cleared the jail of all the scum that weren't paying the gang bosses their money. He crept into their cells in the small hours, slashed his way in through their sheets and shot them in the head as they slept. He was totally ruthless.

Despite making a good rep for himself, he didn't stop bragging about his Rio de Janeiro connections, about how he used to nick Rolexes, and so on, but he really fouled up when he started doing work for both *el Corte Negra* and *el Barrio Chinos*. Both gangs thought he was spending too much time with the other, and you could see it was going to end in disaster.

One night, we heard a huge commotion coming from outside and were told that Joseph had got fresh with one of the daddies. Eight men were dragging him across the yard. They'd dressed him in a red thong and bra, put a red ribbon in his hair and plastered his mouth in red lipstick.

They threw him into a cell with all of the prison's sexual deviants, and we heard that poor lad getting gang-raped, over and over, for what seemed like hours.

The sounds being made weren't human, but we were powerless to help him. To have interfered would have meant the same treatment for us – or death, which probably would have been better.

An hour and a half later, they dragged him back out and took him across to another block where he got more of the same. Anybody who wanted to did him. They raped the fuck out of him.

Eventually, when everybody had finished with him, the gang members threw him into a corner of the outside patio, where he just cowered, shaking and sobbing uncontrollably. He had lipstick everywhere, bite marks all over him.

We never set eyes on him again. For the rest of his time in Yare he never even left his cell. I'd have nightmares about that for a long time after. To hear what I heard and be powerless to help, was horrendous. I don't care what he did; nobody deserved that. Nobody. How could that poor boy ever forget what those bastards put him through? It really was a fate worse than death.

It really affected me and Paul. That night, in my cell, we made a death pact. Paul said, 'If anything like that ever happens to me, I want you to kill me, Jim. Put a bullet through my fucking head, because I would not want to live with that.' We shook hands on it and hugged. I knew he was right. It was one of the many moments when we thought, 'How the hell did our lives ever come to this?'

*

The longer I stayed in Yare, the more I realised just how depraved people could be. I was seeing the very worst of human behaviour. And it had dragged me right down with it. Before all this, I had been just an ordinary, normal lad but in Yare, I'd had to develop a harsh, edgy side to stay alive.

I didn't like the person I'd become. At all.

I was so fucked up that it was around this time that I called my dad and said to him, 'Dad, please don't take this the wrong way, but I don't want you to call me any more. I'm not your son any more. I'm just somebody else here. Please, just forget about me.'

He'd choked up and said, 'Are you sure, son? We want to be here for you, to keep you strong.'

But I'd been firm, and said, 'I want to be left alone. You don't want to hear about the things I've done. I can't hurt you any more.'

It was the most heartbreaking moment of my life, but I had to say it, because my family, my conscience, was getting in the way of what I needed to do to survive. I felt too guilty for some of the things I'd done, but I couldn't talk to them about it because I didn't want to lie to them any more. I figured that what they didn't know couldn't hurt them.

All I knew was that my family was safe, because they were in a safe place, so that was good. But Paul and I weren't. We were in one of the most dangerous places on Earth, and I had to focus everything on my survival.

*

I decided to keep my head down a bit after this and go to work, and I took a job making shoes in a warehouse to keep out of trouble. The shoe-making set-up was run by Eddison, who took me under his wing in his warehouse area. As Eddison was Colombian, most of the fifteen to twenty guys who worked there at any one time were also Colombians. This wasn't just because Eddison was looking after his own, but because working with leather is in the Colombian blood. It's a traditional skill. They made beautiful leather sandals that were sold to order to visitors who came in once a week. We'd each spend about £1.50 on materials from Eddison, then three days later would have a finished pair of sandals we could sell for £5. It was good, skilled work that gave me a focus amongst so much insanity.

But even there, death came randomly knocking once again.

It was the middle of the day, and we were quietly sitting in a row making shoes, when a Colombian guy came in, walked calmly up to a bloke I knew called Gregorio and shot him in the head. We just heard a giant bang, and saw his head jerk back, blood oozing out of him. The episode didn't end there, however, because, instead of keeling over and dying, Gregorio jumped to his feet and ran off, shouting, 'Get out of my way!'

He ran down the central aisle, which was about 100 metres long, with a bullet in his head, did a left, ran another 100 metres, then smacked into a volleyball post, and dropped dead. He was like a newly killed chicken. It really shook me up seeing that. We never did find out why he'd been killed.

Life in Yare was just getting more and more random. Gregorio was the sixth guy I'd seen murdered, right in front of me. How many more would have to die before I was finally free?

Around this time Paul started getting into the Bible. Before Venezuela, he'd never bothered with religion, but there was a priest, Mr Morgan, who visited us regularly, and who made us realise that people did care about us on the outside. It meant the world to us.

I had no more than a casual interest and just read the Bible to be polite, but Paul really got into it and I won't knock him for that. It helped him find strength, and my take on that was, 'Whatever gets you through the day, kid.' Life seemed so chaotic and unfair, believing in a higher power was definitely a better alternative. Paul would say, 'Forgive me, Father, for I have sinned,' and read the book for hours. We needed any driftwood we could cling on to.

While we were in jail, we had to undergo regular psychological screening. Question and answer sessions would happen every couple of months.

The questions were so moronic, a lot of the time I refused to answer them – or deliberately got them wrong to either wind up the psychiatrist or convince him that I was finally losing it.

'What do aeroplanes do?' they'd ask, and I'd reply, 'Serve us gin and tonics.'

They'd reply, 'Mmm, interesting …' and scribble down my reply. Then, 'What noise do they make?' and I'd go, 'You seriously want me to make a fucking aeroplane noise to prove that I'm not mad?'

Then they'd get really daft and ask, 'What shape is an orange?', so I would reply, 'Erm, it's square, innit?'

'Really, you think it's square?'

Of course I fucking didn't! But what did they want me to say? They totally took the piss with that and I couldn't take any more: 'Is that a trick question? Are you taking me for a twat, or what?'

But, just once, it did prove to be useful, as it gave me insight into where my head was at with regards to my family life.

The head doctor had asked me to draw a picture of my family on a blank piece of paper. I found myself drawing my two brothers in the middle, my mum and dad in opposite corners and me far, far away in the background. The guy asked me to analyse it.

I thought for a bit and then said, 'Well, my two brothers are in the middle, because they're back home, see a lot of each other and have a focus. My mum and dad are in opposite corners because they split up. And I'm way back there because I'm far, far away and can't do anything about it.'

He asked me then how, in an ideal world, I'd like the picture to look, and I replied, 'With us all together, in the middle.'

A pretty simple exercise, but it made me realise that one of the major factors for getting involved in this drug smuggling caper was to get away from everything at home: I'd wanted to escape the reality of my life by doing something reckless and free. Well, I'd done that all right, but where had it got me? Locked up in a foreign land, subjected to torture and brutality. It made me hanker after my life back in Blighty once again, and the home-sickness really kicked in. Once again, I had to face up to the terrible stress and heartbreak I'd put my family through, and the shame of my situation being on the TV and in the local newspaper back home. It made me so angry, too, that I had been forced to cut myself off from them, but I'd rather be hurt than harm them any more.

But just when it was all getting a bit heavy, I couldn't resist one final pop at the shrink, who'd finally thought he'd made headway with this stubborn piss-taker.

'I've got one final question for you, James. Why is it you've drawn all of the people as matchstick men?'

I paused, then said, 'Well, my mum and dad are so thin because they're wasting away with worry. It can't be easy for them having a son locked up in Venezuela.' I looked up at him and continued: 'My two little brothers are smaller than me, so I'm gonna make them thin to keep them in their place. They need to know the pecking order in our family. And I'm like a rake because I had to eat a fucking rat last month due to being on hunger strike – not that that did anything for us!'

Needless to say, the shrink's biro went away at that, my folder was closed and I was free to go back to the yard and do something productive, like have a kick-about and a smoke.

It made me wonder what they really hoped to get out of us. I mean, seriously, what did it matter if we thought an orange was purple with pink fucking spots on, or a plane made a mooing noise like a cow? The real reason people were going mad around there was the fact they were getting beaten and shot at by the screws, stabbed or shot by other cons or hiding away from all of life's grimness in a crack pipe. To these very real dangers, though, the authorities just turned a blind eye, and left us to get on with rotting in hell.

CHAPTER 9
ESCAPING FROM HELL

No matter how dangerous it is, prisoners will always try and escape from jails. It's just something to scheme about, something to get excited about and, above all, something to do just to kill the boredom.

We'd made two escape attempts while in La Vega, but they'd only really been half-arsed attempts.

The first time was a bit of a mistake. There were bars in the ceiling above our cell in La Vega, over something a bit like a sky light, and I'd hung a hammock from them. I used to lie there for hours with a blowtorch I'd bought, burning away at these bars, more for something to do than anything else, really.

I was at it again one day when suddenly the whole fucking thing gave way. At first, we were dead excited, but then I said, 'Where the fuck are we going if we get out?' We didn't have a clue where to go, and didn't even have our passports. 'We'd better stop this lark before we get into some serious shit!' We'd shoved it all back up as well as we could, and hoped it would hold.

Then, the last couple of months in La Vega, I made what we called The Famous Hole. With nothing more than a spoon, I'd made a big hole in the wall, where the render was chalky and damp. It was exactly like a scene out of *Shawshank Redemption*. I just kept chopping away and it just kept coming out.

We had no idea where it might even lead to, and in the end the hole got so big, I had to put a poster over it. I pretty much forgot about it until one day, when the governor came round to talk to us, to our horror the poster started flapping a corner in the wind, completely revealing the work I'd been doing. It was so obvious what was going on, God knows how we didn't get caught! Thankfully, we were moved, and they didn't find the hole until after we'd left.

We knew a failed escape attempt was a very serious matter, but for some inmates, escaping became a deadly obsession.

Once, in La Vega, two young men had escaped, but they were apprehended and brought back, battered to fuck and totally naked. To add insult to injury, the police had beaten the shit out of them again, while we were forced to watch. When the guards had finished with them, the two boys had looked almost lifeless.

Another time, a pencil-moustached fella called Armendo, who was a cleaner, and trusted to clean the guards' cells, was let into an outer area where he shouldn't have been, and just buggered off. For two weeks the cops scoured the country. Sure enough, they caught him and brought him back, slinging him back into the cell, bollock naked, before they proceeded to batter him to an absolute pulp. Battered him. They smashed the bones in his hands with the butts of their guns and hammered on him so hard, he was howling out in agony like a scalded dog. Of course, they wouldn't send him to hospital, choosing to just leave him there without so much as an aspirin. Armendo never did recover from that beating, and later became convinced he'd been possessed by a demon. The guards' treatment had sent him mad, and it left us spooked. Being in jail really could send you over the edge and into insanity.

In Yare, two guys actually managed to escape successfully. Their story became the stuff of legend, and encouraged a whole new wave of men to try and bunk out of that hellhole.

The men in question were a pair of bank robbers, a father and son team. The escape rumours centred around the fact that there were about fifteen manhole covers in the prison complex (those that were still there despite the demand for metal for knives, that is) and word had it that the tunnels they covered led to the outside world.

This belief was proved true when the pair made their way out of the prison through the underground network of waste pipes, under the cover of darkness. The word went round Yare like wildfire – there was a manhole cover that definitely 'worked', and which one it was became the talk of endless speculation. Nobody seemed to know.

One night, about two weeks later, twelve lads decided to take their chances down a manhole and escape. When they'd been gone for a week, word spread like wildfire that they'd made it. Every conversation in Yare was tuned to these twelve men. Where had they made it to? Had they killed any National Guards on their way out? Could they, right now, be enjoying themselves in one of Caracas's many whore houses?

Other theories about their fate, however, were more sinister.

The communal kitchen was a grim place, and we never used to eat in there unless we had to. It was only open whenever meagre supplies showed up and sometimes it was days between prepared meals. When the cry went up for food there was an unholy charge for the kitchen, with fights breaking out among the poorest bastards who ate there. Basically, if you could afford to buy your own food and stay away you did.

But if you were forced to eat there, there were no plates, so if you didn't have your own you had to snap a mango leaf off a tree and make do with that. Worse, the tables were long, concrete affairs that were covered in food slops that were never cleaned off. You didn't even want to sit down there, let alone eat there. The whole place buzzed with flies, while on top of the tables sat most of the prison's dog population, waiting to be thrown morsels or just snaffle food off before they could be shooed away.

Anyway, one day, not long after the twelve had escaped, a rumour went round that a guy had said he'd looked into a big pot bubbling away in the kitchens and seen 'swine flesh' – slang for human meat.

Tales of cannibalism and human sacrifice were rife in Venezuela, as human meat was meant to have mythical properties among some religious sects. Venezuela is mostly Catholic, but the worship of other gods and cults is commonplace in the remote countryside, where super- stition and legend still reigns.

One of the creepiest cannibalism stories I ever heard in prison came from a pimp. Antonio was a blond-haired lad who always had three girls on the go at any one time and a wicked cell full of all the top gear, like CD players, a TV and even game consoles. He also had a great line in stories, and told us about a sacred mountain in Venezuela called Sorte where human sacrifices were rife – and the locals ate the tributes afterwards.

Antonio filled us in one evening: 'The area is heavily guarded by the National Guard, but they will let you in if you bribe them. As you drive up the mountain, you get so far until you come to a brook you have to cross by foot. When you're halfway across, for good luck you flip a coin behind you, and even though it lands in the water, and you can see the splash, the noise it makes sounds like it's landed on a marble floor. It is the creepiest noise you will ever hear, and it signifies you are entering sacred and magical ground.' Antonio looked around at us all, to make sure we were listening. Our ears were flapping. 'Then you carry on walking, and suddenly, you will feel a snake wrap around you. This snake, it licks your face, then unwraps itself and goes. If you survive, it signifies that you have been accepted by the gods, and can carry on.' Perhaps in the cold light of day, the story sounds over the top, but at the time, it was electric, part of the culture we found ourselves in. 'Keep going, and you will meet a local, who will take you to the sacred village, but only if you take him a soul. You have to take him a person, for him to sacrifice.' Antonio paused, enjoying the look on our faces. 'It's what all the bad boys do. If somebody does them over for a few dollars, what do they do? They're going to kill them anyway, but these natives will sacrifice them for you, and it is meant to bring good luck. They grind down the bones and eat the flesh. There is nothing left of anybody who goes up there.'

He swore it was true. I asked Kiki when she next came to see Paul, and she said it was true. It freaked me out, but I still didn't really believe it. Then one day I was watching the news and a story came on about Dorangel Vargas. He was known as *el Comegente* – Spanish for 'people-eater' – and was a serial killer and cannibal. He'd killed and eaten at least ten people, and cops had found loads of human remains in his farm on the outskirts of Caracas. He'd been killing and eating people for years. I was shocked, but the Venezuelans took it in their stride. To them, cannibalism was just another part of their mad country's history.

But serving up man-flesh to us for dinner was taking the piss. Word spread fast that human hot-pot was on the menu that night, and that it was made of the twelve men who'd tried to escape. The Chinese-whisper fire-balled, and pretty soon everybody in Yare believed that the men had been caught, cut up and put into the prison food to teach the twelve men – and everybody else – a stomach-turning lesson in tough justice. Nobody ate that night.

The next morning, however, we learned that something far worse had happened to those twelve lads. As we filed out to wash, we were greeted by a truly horrific sight. In front of us, piled up in a big stack, were the dead bodies of all twelve men. Their skin had gone all yellow and was hanging off their bloated bodies, which were completely battered, as if they'd been smashed against walls and all sorts.

They had obviously been dead some time, and now they were outside in the heat, they stank to high heaven. It was putrid.

The guards didn't say a word about how they'd caught the men and, once again, Yare's rumour mill went into overdrive. One theory was that they'd made it into the outside world, only to be apprehended by National Guards and packs of their dogs, who'd shot, mauled and beaten them to death in the desert, then dragged them back to make an example of them. Another rumour gave me nightmares. Word had it that the doomed men had gone down the wrong manhole, and had come to a dead end in the tunnel that had flooded after heavy rain. They'd all drowned together, then decayed underwater until the floods subsided, at which point the sewer rats had moved in and feasted on their corpses.

Whatever it was, this dirty dozen weren't getting anywhere near a parole hearing any time soon.

It was horrendous. These men had been so driven to despair by life in Yare, they'd died trying to escape. Death, it seemed, was the only way of escaping this forgotten valley where the devil danced.

I got so desperate to get out of there, too, that I seriously contemplated shooting or stabbing myself.

I was sitting in Eddison's cell, completely depressed, when I said to him, 'How the fuck can I get out of here?'

Eddison replied that it was probably easiest to escape from hospitals outside the prison.

Nobody went to hospital if they could help it, if the screws would let you in the first place, because part of the process was that you had to be interrogated by the National Guard and explain who it was that had wounded you. Of course, the punishment for grassing up another con was certain death, so we patched ourselves up the best we could and got by without medical treatment.

And that's when Eddison said, 'You've got a gun. Shoot yourself in the fucking foot, *compadre*!'

At first, I'd laughed. It was like some World War I story from the trenches of the Somme. But then I thought: How much would it hurt, really? I'd wanted to take my own life playing Russian roulette, so what was a blasted foot between friends? After all, I could always get some hardcore painkillers, drink a bottle of rum and get Eddison to pull the trigger.

After a bit of to-ing and fro-ing, however, Eddison flatly refused in case word got out that it was him that had done it, and even though I pointed my Beretta at my foot, I just couldn't do it.

Instead, I took my knife and grabbed a roll of flesh from my waist, but I knew that sticking myself there would look like I'd stabbed myself. I couldn't risk stabbing myself through an organ, or nicking a bone. Eddison suggested I stab my leg, but I'd seen people die of blood loss after a knife wound to a major artery in the leg, as it took so long for the guards to get to you.

Finally, Paul turned to me and just said, 'Jim, leave it.'

I'd replied, 'But we could go home!'

He just looked at me sadly and said, 'The only way you'll go home if you stab or shoot yourself is in a fucking coffin, kid.'

It was horrific and disrespectful how the guards treated the dead in Yare. It was as if the dead had never been human beings at all. To those bastards, bodies were just lumps of meat. And when Eddison was treated in the same way, it broke our hearts. He had been shot dead at 8 a.m. on a Wednesday morning while shaving, for allegedly grassing on a geezer years ago in a different nick. Who knew? Eddison certainly didn't. Sometimes, when death came knocking, it meant nothing. Nobody ever even knew who did it.

They shot Eddison twice: once through the neck, and once through his torso, then left him to bleed to death on the floor. When the guards found him, they stuck him on a trolley, threw a sheet over him, tied it down with a couple of bungee cords and left him out in the baking heat by reception.

Dignity was a rare commodity in Yare. In fact, it seemed practically non-existent.

It was visiting time, and Eddison's wife had come to see him that day. His body lay on that trolley in full view of the queue of visitors. His eyes were open and he still had shaving foam on his face. I can see that image even now. His wife was looking at this body, and she couldn't see who it was, but we watched her come in through the gate, and saw as the guards told her what had happened to her husband and pointed to Eddison's corpse.

We watched that woman's heart break.

Fair enough, the guards made it their mission to break us. But the collateral damage meant that others – family and friends – were all too often left devastated by the guards' casual brutality, too. It made us think again of the pain we'd inflicted on our own families.

A little while after this, we heard that the two bank robbers, the father and son, were eventually caught; not while on the run, but while carrying out another bank robbery. They'd done all the hard work, but couldn't stay free because they didn't know about anything else other than robbing banks. This time, they weren't sent to Yare: they knew the way out. No, they were sent to El Rodeo, another notorious jail that was thought much harder to escape from on account of the fact it had a crocodile- and piranha-infested lagoon around it.

The manhole escape route was finally fucked up when Ayala was caught trying to use it. He only had two years of his sentence left to run and had a cushy job in the prison's sub-station, but had got it into his head that he had to escape. Word got out that he was going to attempt it, and he was watched. Unwittingly, he led the guards right to the (correct) manhole cover. He got a severe beating for his troubles and was transferred to another jail. One of my closest friends in Yare was gone, and I was lost without him.

* * *

Despite doubts about what life in Yare was doing to me, businesswise, Paul and I were doing well. I was the fixer and the enforcer, while Paul was the calming influence and the brains. We were the perfect team. We controlled the drug trade in the Annexo, we had good guns, we had machetes, a protection network and a room to stash everything.

We'd got good jobs working in the governor's kitchen, helping a mate of ours to prepare the guards' meals. It gave us a bit of extra cash, and we got to eat good food. The only thing that could fuck things up for us now was a police set-up.

I used to chop peppers; that was my part of the deal and, in return, we would hide huge quantities of drugs and our arsenal in the kitchen's cupboards. Because of the chef's connection to the authorities, the room never got searched.

Or so we thought.

One day, about eighteen months into our stay at Yare, a fat, slippery copper we used to call *Mantequilla* – 'butter' – walked into the room where we were working. Well, we called him a copper, but he was in fact a vigilante – a local who was paid to police the prison. Men like him made up a large part of the prison security. The National Guards were the 'official' security outfit.

'Hey, boys, I've got a kilo of weed for sale at a special price,' he said.'Do you want it? £80 and it's yours.'

Does a bear shit in the woods? It would be a sure-fire money-spinner for us: we could off-load all this dope within one day and double our money.

Trouble was, Mantequilla was a grade-A twat. He'd once killed a prisoner by shooting him at point-blank range with his shotgun, completely blowing his chest out with a plastic bullet, so we were wary. But greed got the better of us. This deal was a steal.

'Yeah, yeah, bring it on,' we said.

So he went off and came back with this great big bag of stinky weed. This bush was massive, the real McCoy. Me and Paul wasted no time in chopping it up – the kitchen worktop gave us much more room to work with.

We decided to cut it into smaller deals and wrap it in squares of newspaper, into what we called five wraps – roughly the same as an eighth of an ounce deal in the UK. We didn't have scales, but experience had taught us exactly how big the deals needed to be. Not too big so you're cutting profits, but not too small so angry punters would cut your throat.

As we were banging the gear out, Paul started thinking. 'This doesn't feel right,' he said. 'What if we get caught with all this shit?'

I urged him to chill out, and assured him it'd be OK, saying, 'Let's just crack on and let's get this over with, quick.'

All of a sudden, four knocks came on the door, with a pause between knocks two and three. It was part of our secret knock we'd devised with our pal the chef. That way, we'd never accidentally open the door – which we'd locked from the inside – to enemies or guards. There were supposed to be two final taps at the end of our special knock, but they didn't come.

In the resulting panic, I told Paul it was OK too soon. When he opened the door, who was standing there? Two fucking coppers and the kitchen table still covered with little bits of weed.

Reaching over, one of the guards took a cigarette out of my pocket, taking his time as he surveyed the scene. 'Well, well, well, and what do we have here, boys?' he asked.

We were caught bang to rights. There'd be no wriggling out of this one, so I tried to lighten the situation: 'What does it look like? It's about a kilo of marijuana.'

He smirked. 'And what, my friend, are you going to do with that?'

'I'm going to light a big bong up and smoke it, what do you think?'

I grinned, reluctantly resigned to the fact that we'd been nicked. I also wondered if we'd be able to give them a cut and they'd let us off. It had happened many times in the past; it was all part of the shakedown corrupt guards went through to boost their meagre pay.

But I was mistaken. These bastards were giving us the full treatment, and would show us no mercy. They not only took all the dope, but they started a search of the whole sodding room. When they'd finished that, they moved on to our cells. They found all my guns and four machetes under my mattress, plus a big stash of charlie. They took the whole fucking lot.

This wasn't good. 'Look, take the drugs, fair deal,' I pleaded with them. 'But you can't take my armour – it's our protection. We'll be dead.'

The guard thought for a moment. 'OK, you'll get it back if we get £200 by 2 p.m.,' he replied.

We knew we couldn't get our hands on that sort of money at such short notice. We'd been set up. Totally stitched. The wanker who'd sold us the drugs had gone straight to these other guards and told them to come and bust us. The worst of it was that these thieving bastards would probably go and sell the drugs again to somebody else, and shake them down, too, for the same kind of money. That kind of bollocks was commonplace: cops would sell and confiscate the same consignment of drugs several times, making many times its value while they were at it; not to mention profiting from selling all the other stuff they got, like the guns and other weapons.

But it had never happened to us before. We'd always paid off all the right people and played with a straight bat.

Sure enough, an hour later, I went to Ramon, a guy I normally got my weed off, and he was selling exactly the same drugs the cops had just taken off us. It was even wrapped in the same fucking newspaper!

'Where did you get this?' I asked.

'I just bought it for £80 off Butter,' he replied.

'That's the same as I paid an hour ago – off the same fucking cop!' I told him. Butter had made £160 from a kilo, plus there'd be another £200 on top that he'd make selling all my confiscated weapons. Not bad for a day's work when you only earn £30 a month.

It left us in the shit. Weapons-wise, we were back to square one and dangerously exposed. We had no choice but to go to the Black Cut and borrow money to buy new guns – we'd have been dead within a day without them. It would mean crippling interest rates, but a stiff loan is better than, well, being a stiff.

I approached Butter the next day and said, 'Right, fair enough. Yesterday you got us. But you know we will get guns again. I want you to tell me you won't pull the same stunt again.'

'We knew you had guns all along,' he boasted. 'That's why we searched you. You've got plenty of money. You're loaded, and waltz around like you own the place. You had to be kept in line.'

'You've got it all wrong,' I said, through gritted teeth. 'Just don't go searching us again, because you know that would be wrong.'

The prison had many 'unofficial rules', especially when it came to the vigilantes, but Butter was seriously breaking them. They supplied us with drugs, guns, knives, booze, women and food – basically anything we asked for. And in return we had to do our utmost not to be caught with contraband items by the National Guard. The vigilantes did have the power to search us and confiscate anything they found. On occasions the more corrupts ones would abuse our unspoken agreement, by supplying illegal items only for a random search to be thrown minutes later. And this was exactly what Butter had done now. 'You know me, boys,' he smirked. 'I like to play by the rules. Anyway, don't worry. You *gringos* are being moved soon. We just wanted to make sure we took all your shit off you before you left us.'

'We're getting moved?' I asked. 'It's the first we've fucking heard.'

'After what you did to Seven Necks, the governor thinks you're getting too wild,' Butter said.

I didn't care about that, as something had just occurred to me: 'If we're getting moved, why the fuck did you try and sell us our stuff back for £200, knowing we wouldn't be able to take it with us, anyway?' I fumed.

'You know how it is,' replied the slippery bastard, laughing in my face. 'A man's got to make a living.'

And that's how we learned we were leaving Yare. Not in the way you might hope – by finding out at court, or via a letter from the prison authorities, or even a visit from a British Embassy official. It was a fitting end to our time in what is surely the most corrupt and insane jail on earth.

The following morning, we were marched to the governor's office. After a short lecture, he finished up by laughing, 'You were very naughty, my friend.' At that moment, Seven Necks came walking in, while, earlier that day, I heard later, Lachuga had been in to see the boss, with a towel wrapped around him, looking really ill.

I realised I'd been grassed up by two of my enemies.

We were told that we were being moved to a jail called El Junquito.

The only person who knew anything about El Junquito was an inmate I'd met who we called the Terrorist. He was a good-looking, chubby little fella, with immaculately shampooed hair and Tommy Hilfiger shirts. He was also a rich, very intelligent Venezuelan who was well connected and powerful, and who was doing time after he tried to blow up one of the former presidents of Venezuela. He'd been to university in America, was fluent in the language and heavily involved in revolutionary Communist politics.

You could tell he had dough, as he had access to some top weaponry, too. One day, he came in with some C4 plastic explosive he'd had smuggled in. It was an off-yellow colour and he told me he wanted to put it on the governor's door. He pointed to the governor's quarters, and said, 'I'll blow that door off, and the blast will suck back through the whole unit. You will see the governor's head just fucking *go*! Shall we do it for a laugh?'

He was also paranoid as fuck, mainly because he smoked more crack than I've ever seen one man do. When he had a visit from his blonde, gorgeous German wife, he'd always come back with £80 worth of crack that she had smuggled in. Even by Yare's standards, £80 was a serious amount of crack. I could have tripled or even quadrupled my money on that and it would have kept me alive for a month in prison. But this guy used to smoke it in one night.

Another time, I saw him steam through £240 worth of cocaine and crack in one sitting with a few friends, which is one serious drug binge. It had its drawbacks, though – serious paranoia.

The National Guards paraded at night outside his cell. They always carried a flashing red beacon to mark their position, but the Terrorist became convinced the flashing red light was a camera, or a sniper rifle that was trained on him. Panicking, he'd turned to me, saying, 'Look, Jim! The red light, it's on me again! It's dancing on my chest!'

I had calmed him down, but then he said, 'Jim, chop me some of that cookie off. If I'm going to die, I might as well do it high. But get down on the floor, first! If they see you with me, they'll shoot you, too!' I finally convinced him there was nobody there, but he still sat in his little shorts sweating his tits off and ploughing through that pile of crack.

Well, the Terrorist told us we had finally got lucky. 'El Junquito … it's the most comfortable jail in the whole country. That's where the fucking corrupt pig ex-president served time.'

The Terrorist knew his politics and told us that Carlos Andres Perez, the corrupt president that Hugo Chavez attacked, had been sent there when he was kicked out of power and accused of mass corruption and murdering many of his political enemies. He was also found guilty of siphoning off up to £25 million from public funds during his four-year presidency. For his sins, he was sentenced to a mere two years' porridge, but was let out after serving only a few months.

We were made up. It was January, the start of a new year, and we were filled with fresh optimism. Finally, it seemed we'd got a lucky break and would get to a comfy jail at last.

After all, if El Junquito was good enough for an ex-president, it was good enough for us.

CHAPTER 10

REFORMED MEN

We left Yare in the evening, just as it was starting to get dusky. We stood waiting at the gates for two hours, with our mattresses tied up with string under our arms. We knew the guards were watching us like hawks from their towers, and would shoot us if we so much as moved.

A van eventually arrived and picked us up, and we went back through Caracas, past La Planta jail, making our way higher up into the mountains.

The night, added to the altitude, meant it was much cooler, and for the first time in Venezuela we were actually cold. It oddly felt really good after so many months of stinking heat.

During the trip, our mood was buoyant. 'We're going to a nice nick,' I said to Paul. 'That must mean they're going to set us free soon. Why else would they send us there?'

*

El Junquito was situated in Caracas itself. It was a small nick, with only about fifty men in it at any one time. It was like a category-C jail, so most offenders you got there were only in for relatively minor crimes, like fraud or forging passports or banknotes.

On arrival, it was dark. We were made to sleep in a room in the back. When we asked if we could see the jail, the guards just said, 'Tomorrow.'

The next morning – after the first quiet night's sleep in a long time – an Italian guy who looked like a complete nerd came into the cell. He didn't look like he'd say 'Boo' to anyone. In fact, he looked really sad, and didn't speak a word of Spanish or English, apart from, 'In shampoo! In bag!', which he kept repeating.

We figured he was either a bit of a nutter or wanted some shampoo, but it turned out that he had been busted for drug smuggling, so was in the same shit as us, and the last remnants of his booty was two thumbs – twenty grams – of cocaine that he'd stashed in his shampoo, which was being held by the guards.

We asked a few people in there to get hold of his stuff for him from reception, and when they did, amazingly the guards hadn't searched his shampoo. And that's how we got started in El Junquito.

After all we'd been through in La Vega and Yare, it was just instinct to seize a chance to make money and acquire weapons at the earliest opportunity.

Still unsure about what to expect, the first time we went out in air, into the yard, we were approached by a huge black guy. When he spoke to us, I could tell he was educated. I'd spent so much time with Venezuelans of all classes by this time that I understood who spoke slang, and who had upbringing. Like Luis the tattooist in Yare, I knew this fella was middle class. He was polite, and we knew a lot of each other's friends from previous jails.

This was the beginning of my feelings of complete culture shock. El Junquito prison had a totally different feel to the ones we were used to. The first few weeks at El Junquito, in fact, I went around feeling totally emotional that people were actually being nice to us. We'd been treated like scum for so long, we just didn't think we deserved anything else than a good kicking. I'd had so much of my goodness kicked out of me, it was like a part of my heart had been burned out.

The prison was occupied by inmates who actually wanted to talk, and help each other. It was a well-funded prison, where inmates cooked nice food, had a laugh, listened to music and watched movies together.

The food was gorgeous: fresh veggies and decent meat like shredded steak – not a rat in sight! – and people queued in an orderly way. They even said sorry if they knocked into you.

Finally, we felt we could relax a bit. El Junquito was a very progressive prison. It worked. The system worked. Treat cons with respect and they start to behave: there were no knives and I never once saw a gun in there.

There was no need for them. If people had a beef, they sorted it out English-style – with fists – and that was that. But violence was very rare.

Of course, there were still drugs, but mainly everybody just smoked weed and chilled out while watching films. You got the odd coke head, but they were very much in the minority.

About two months into our time in El Junquito, I realised I was changing. By this time, I felt half-Venezuelan. I'd begun to respect the guys we were living beside: they had compassion, and I liked the way they behaved. They'd share their last mouthful of food, even if they would stab you for drugs or money.

There was a church in the jail, and I'd go with Paul. There was also a professor in there who lent us books, and I read up on Venezuelan history, which I found fascinating. I really got into the story of Simon Bolivar, one of the early military leaders who fought against the Spanish for South American independence. It was nice to feel relaxed enough to read a book. But beyond that, I was gaining a profound respect for Venezuela and its struggles in the past. To understand a country's history is to understand its people, and I figured every little insight might help me survive.

Our spirits were further boosted because our girlfriends, Siyanni and Kiki, were still able to come and visit us. There was also a proper dentist there – unlike the

Invented Dentist – and I finally got some teeth sorted that had been giving me aggro for ages.

Good things were happening. Even the guards were reasonable in El Junquito. There was nowhere to weight-train, which was annoying as I'd got really into weights in Yare and La Vega as a way of working off stress and staying fit and sane. However, I soon heard that one of the guards had a set of homemade weights in his quarters. Although he was initially frosty, he soon started letting me use his concrete weights, and we struck up a decent relationship.

Christ, even the guards had hearts! To me and Paul, it was totally alien. We were used to living in fear of violent attack from both cons and guards, by stabbings or copping a bullet in your head. In fact, at first, we thought it was a set-up, some kind of sick trick, and that any minute the guards would wade into us, swords flailing. After all we'd been through, we'd practically lost all faith in human nature, and that made me really sad. But, finally, I felt like I had a chance here, and I vowed to change my ways. I promised myself to give up violence, to stop acting like a caged animal. Before, rage and anger had been all that had got me through. Now, I genuinely wanted to change, serve my time and get home to my family a changed, wiser and better man. It wouldn't be an easy thing to do and I found I still needed to smoke weed to help me make the transition. It had become a part of my way of life by now and everybody else in there liked to smoke, too. But I decided to do away with the hard drugs and no longer carry knives or guns.

One guy, a real loner called Jenkins, had caught my eye early on, as he looked like the sort of bloke who could flip, he was so quiet. I decided to approach him and ask him his story but he wouldn't tell me, and I knew enough about volatile and violent cons not to push them. In jail as in life, it's always the quiet ones you should look out for. But there was something about Jenkins that intrigued me, and every few days I'd persist, even telling him my story in an attempt to get him to open up.

It was during one of these chats outside one day that he suddenly said: 'Watch the tennis ball! Don't touch it!'

I didn't have a fucking clue what he was on about, until a tennis ball came flying over the prison wall and landed in the yard.

The jail was overlooked by mountains, built into the sides of which were lots of houses. We were well used to locals throwing things in at us. As the only *gringos* in there, Paul and I had developed quite a fan club of local girls, who used to call us The Backstreet Boys and throw us their knickers. But the guards had always said to us, 'Do not touch. Drugs.'

This was the first time I'd seen a tennis ball come over like this, and it was obvious that it was a way for cons to get narcotics into the nick. I found it quite funny that as we spoke, out there beyond the prison walls, one of the con's drug dealers was twatting tennis balls full of goodies from the boot of his car with a tennis racquet.

Jenkins carried on. 'As soon as you touch the ball, the coppers will get you. They will open the balls and find cocaine, or cannabis, and they will pin it on you. Never touch the tennis balls.'

I looked around and a group of cons with hungry eyes were staring at the ball like it was the most important thing on earth. But none of them moved a muscle – they all knew the drill. Sure enough, fifteen minutes later, a cop came over, picked up the ball, pulled it apart and fished out a bag of white powder. He held it between two fingers, flapping it to the cons, agonisingly out of their reach.

This moment broke the ice with Jenkins, who finally trusted me enough to tell me his tale. He started to speak, baldly and unemotionally.

'I do not care if I am in here for the rest of my life. I have got nothing on the outside. I had a daughter, she was fifteen, nice-looking girl. She went around to her friend's one day, and her father and his friends, they decided they were going to rape her. After, she committed suicide. Her friend told me her dad had done this to my beloved daughter, and I went round to the block, and I killed everyone there.'

At that, he crossed himself, and went on.

'I went in there with two mini guns, and as many grenades as I could carry. I shot everybody I saw, and blew up floors. It was a massacre, Jim. But I did not give a fuck. They told me I killed at least seventy people in there.'

His story explained what had made me notice him early on. He lived in a focused world of his own – every day he relived what had happened to his daughter. He was still trooping on that land. It made me feel immensely sad, yet very close to him. It was the most heartbreaking story I'd ever heard any con come out with – and I'd heard hundreds of hard-luck tales. To go that far for your child was mind-blowing, and I felt honoured he'd chosen to open up to me and share his unimaginable grief.

Although lots of innocent people had died in the fall-out of Jenkins' actions, he seemed oddly at peace with himself that his daughter's rapists had been vanquished. It made my own problems seem insignificant in comparison, and any thoughts of me and Paul feeling sorry for ourselves were gone in the face of his troubles.

Jenkins never got into a single piece of trouble in El Junquito. He was above such petty concerns. His distance, his serene calmness; it was almost other-wordly. It gave him power, and people often went to him for advice. He was the daddy who never once got his hands dirty, as his story and reputation meant he was covered. The dude was like our Yoda.

My relationship with Jenkins reminded me that it wasn't all grim in Venezuelan jails. It might sound hard to understand against the backdrop of violence, murder, guns, gang warfare and drugs, but I had some of the most meaningful times of my life in those nicks. You get really close to people in jail in a way you never do in the outside world, because your life depends on them. Because you're in the shit together and have a common enemy in the system, you become more like brothers than friends. When somebody is prepared to die for you – or actually kills a man for you – it goes way beyond having a pint and a game of pool with the lads down the boozer on a Friday night. I can understand why, for many men, jail is somewhere they come to regard as the place they belong, a system they're successful in, and they find life outside on the streets just doesn't have the same meaning. Out there, they're just another number. But inside they can be a face, a daddy who commands authority. It gives them a self-respect they'd never have if they were on the outside, skint and just another jobless nobody. I saw men coming and going from jail like yo-yos and, often, they were really happy to be back inside, to catch up with old friends and make new ones.

Although El Junquito was a place with a lot less prison crap going on, we still had to go for regular psychiatric assessments. There, we were actually happy to go to as many as possible – not because we thought we were going mad, but because the female doctors were well fit!

One day, I was taken to an office for another assessment, and the room was unbelievable. It turned out that this was where ex-president Perez had been locked up when he was kicked out of power. He'd taken over the governor's quarters and had it converted into his 'cell'. The entire room was lined with black marble, with gold in between the tiles. The chairs were made of oxblood leather, all the furniture was dark, solid oak and there was a balcony that overlooked a swimming pool. It was one serious room, one that would have graced the world's finest hotel, never mind a prison cell for a murderous dictator. It was a level of luxury you would never expect to see in Venezuela.

In El Junquito, Paul and I got closer again. In La Vega, we'd shared a cell and practically lived in each other's pockets. But in Yare, we'd drifted apart. He'd decided he didn't want anything to do with all the violence, and had stayed in his cell for weeks at a time, reading the Bible. But I had wanted to be outdoors, playing football, dealing drugs, pulling triggers and fighting.

Now, we pulled together as brothers. We respected each other again. And finally, we really focused on getting our heads down and organising our paperwork. With the help of Siyanni and Kiki, we started building our files and getting all the right documents together.

To have any chance of getting a pardon, there were several things we'd have to do. First, we'd have to prove we'd paid our way inside by working. I'd been making papier maché vases, sandals and light shades out of lollipop sticks, all of which the prisoners sold to visitors when they came in.

I used to love those shades. You made them look like a globe, with a light inside, and when it rotated, it flickered. It took about 1,000 lollipop sticks and a week to do, but you could flog them for £8 a pop. They were a big hit, and in El Junquito, I was making them to order. It was something to do, and it got you positive feedback for your paperwork, which was vital if we ever wanted to get out on remand.

We also had to show that we'd been behaving ourselves. While Paul taught English, I'd joined the prison football team, and taken up boxing and weight-training again. The only problem with the football team was that I wasn't allowed to leave the nick to travel to away games like the rest of the team, as I was considered too much of a security risk.

When I complained, the guards told me, 'If the local boys try and escape, we will shoot them. But if we shoot you, we will have Amnesty International up our asses, so screw you.' There wasn't a lot I could say to that.

We also had to study, and so Paul and I would go to classes up on the hill and take maths classes and IT. And, every night between 7 and 9 p.m., we'd go and listen to a history lecture. Our noses had never been cleaner, in or out of prison!

We had arrived in El Junquito thinking the authorities had thought we'd learned our lesson and had been through enough shit. We'd been told by the Embassy that we were to serve out the rest of our sentence there, and then get released.

But, as so often happened, Fate dealt us a cruel blow.

About three months after we had arrived there, one of the guards told us we were all due to get kicked out into other jails, because the government had had a change of plan, and wanted to change El Junquito into a parole jail.

Sure enough, one day the guards came in and shouted for a roll call. When we had all lined up, they pointed to a group of us, and said 'La Planta'. A van pulled up, and we were shoved into it. We didn't even have time to pack.

Once again, we were being shifted to another jail, handcuffed and under armed guard like the world's most wanted terrorists.

For four long hours, we bounced along in the back of a sweatbox on wheels, back into the stinking, third-world squalor of Caracas.

On the way to La Planta on that day in March 2000, three and a half years into our sentence, I was nervous for a variety of reasons. In El Junquito, we'd had a taste of civility. We'd been treated with respect and it had softened us. Now we were heading to La Planta, the place my dad had warned me to avoid as he'd seen inmates openly walking around with grenades and guns on display. We really felt like we were going back to square one. We had also heard that just the week before, twenty-eight men had been killed in a mass riot that had culminated in the police throwing hand grenades into cells in a ham-fisted and desperate attempt to restore order. And, finally, it had dawned on me that I'd finally have to face an old adversary, in the shape of Patrick, the African prince I'd mugged back in La Vega. I'd taken about £80 off him and smashed his radio when he'd refused to turn down his deafening music.

Just before I'd left Yare, I'd shared a cell with a lad called Christian, who'd been transferred in from La Planta. Totally by chance, it turned out that while in La Planta, he'd been Patrick's right-hand man, performing the heavy-handed shit like stabbings and shootings. He had confirmed rumours I'd already heard – that Patrick was building his arsenal and wanted me dead.

Christian had warned me, 'Every time somebody mentioned your name in La Planta, Patrick would say, "I want that guy dead." He said it to anybody who would listen.' Apparently, as far as Patrick was concerned, Paul was all right, and the word was that if we got moved to La Planta, he was to be looked after. But – 'Kill Jim. I will pay the man well who murders that fuck for me.'

Christian had made the point that no one else in La Planta knew me, except Patrick, and 'he's given you a bad name, that you're the fucker, and that nobody should trust you'.

I didn't need this shit. It seemed it just would not go away. Like many wronged lags, it seemed this prick Patrick had a memory like an elephant: he never forgot.

I'd known that I'd have to deal with him right away if I was ever moved to La Planta and in the three months I shared a cell with Christian, I had made sure I got to know Patrick's every move: where he hung out in La Planta, who stood with him, who disliked him. I learned he was making a living selling beads, of all things – he'd gone legit.

Then Christian gave me information that was to prove crucial to my survival. 'When it comes down to it, Patrick is a shit bag,' he'd said. 'He gets other people like me to do his dirty work. But if you don't pull that trigger for him, he won't do anything about it. He's not got the balls. Get to him and confront him directly, and I think he will shit his pants and leave you alone. But you will have to strike fast.'

I realised this was top advice. With Patrick, it was all front. He might have been a leader in his own country, but in Venezuela he wasn't anything. I, however, had made it in the country on my own terms. I had the advantage over him and decided that attack would be the best form of defence.

We finally arrived at the jail, which was made up of huge, ugly concrete blocks in the middle of Caracas. La Planta was a good, old-fashioned shit heap, full of good, old-fashioned, murderous scum. It was time to face the music in this new hell.

We were used to getting shit the minute we walked into a new jail in Venezuela. We'd been mugged in La Vega and I had been threatened with stabbing within moments of getting to Yare, and I already knew what aggro I'd get in La Planta.

Added to this, Christian had told me, 'When you move to La Planta, the authorities give everybody a skinhead – a real good shave – whether you like it or not.'

I hadn't liked the sound of that, and thought I'd kick up a stink about it. At the time, I'd grown dreadlocks and had beads in my hair, so I decided to pretend I'd converted to Jah, a Jamaican cult. I planned to tell the authorities at La Planta that dreadlocks were a fundamental part of my beliefs, just to try and flout the system and score a small moral victory. It might sound daft, but in jail every little point scored against the authorities was a major triumph that kept you sane. To be honest, I was also just quite attached to my dreads.

My story didn't count for anything, however. The guards didn't even bother to listen to my bullshit story about Jah and the religious importance of my dreadlocks: two burly guys just sat me down on a crate and, woof, shaved the whole lot off.

With that indignity out of the way, we were shoved through into the reception area, and we caught our first glimpse of the nick for real. We could just see row after row of cells through the bars; the cells only screened from each other by sheets the cons had hung for a little privacy.

It was then that I received my first veiled threat from Patrick. A guy came over to the bars of his cell and said through them, 'Gringo, Patrick says hello. You will be seeing him very soon.'

We hadn't even got inside the gaff and it had started. Patrick knew I was here, and his spots had already clocked me. It meant word would be back to him before I had even stepped foot into my new cell.

Suddenly, I decided I was bored of the whole thing. Threats are all part and parcel of jails, but where was the action? If I had wanted somebody as badly as Patrick made out he wanted me, I'd have arranged for a grenade to have gone off by now. I felt a bit better.

We were led to a cell. As I looked down the corridor, with its row after row of cells, all I could see were gun barrels poking out through the bars. After what seemed like a break at El Junquito, we were back to another shit house full of tooled-up murderers.

Right by the door to our cell, I could see a pair of black arms hanging out from between the bars, and I knew they were Patrick's. I looked over and muttered to Paul, 'Patrick's in there, look. What the fuck? They're putting us in with the cunt!'

The guards – who no doubt had been bribed – had put us in the cell next door to the guy who everybody in the whole fucking place knew wanted me dead.

I asked the guard if we could move, but he replied coldly, 'No. You must go in there.'

Patrick, however, didn't say anything. He just retreated into his cell. For now, we were spared a confrontation.

There are times in jail when inmates have to be patient. They might have to wait months before a guy they want to get revenge on is on his own, unprotected by his crew. Or, a wanted man might hide indoors for years until he takes that fateful stroll in the yard and gets the bullet with his name on it. Patience is usually always rewarded, and acting rashly before the right moment can get you killed. But there are other times when you have to act fast. Fast, as in your-life-depends-on-it fast. Now was one of those times.

There was an obvious way I could protect myself from Patrick: with my own weapons. The trouble was, we got to La Planta with nothing. All the arsenal we'd amassed in Yare had been seized before we left. All we'd got to our names were our toothbrushes. Of course, we could always buy weapons, but we wouldn't get our hands on any money until our first Embassy visit in a few days' time.

To make matters worse, we'd heard in Yare that when you got to La Planta you had to pay £100 a month for protection. I'd decided, however, that we didn't want any protection – and we definitely weren't paying for it.

Now, Paul argued with me, saying: 'Of course we've got to pay for protection. What are you going to do if one of these cunts comes at you with a gun or a knife? Offer to clean his fucking teeth?'

We laughed about it, but I still decided we'd take our chances on our own – and use the £100 we 'saved' to buy knives. We'd built ourselves up from nothing before and ended up with a whole bunch of guns. I was sure we could do it again.

It was fair to say the situation had me fucking pissed off. We hadn't got a pot to piss in, there was a guy in the next cell who wanted to murder me, we'd got to pay £100 for stupid protection we didn't even want and, on top of it all, I'd been shaved as bald as a whore's fanny.

Just when the day couldn't get any worse, I saw this black arm beckon me over. Patrick's arm. That's when I thought, 'Fuck it, I'm just gonna stick it to that bastard, I've had enough.' I'd got used to the quiet life at El Junquito, and I'd started becoming the person I wanted to be again. I'd become calmer and learned to press the pause button when anger kicked in. I listened to Paul more, who made me see that violence was the fool's way out and that talking was a better remedy. But fuckers like Patrick just wouldn't leave me alone, and it made me see red.

Paul tried to calm me down, saying, 'I'll talk to him. He's not violent, he'll listen.' But I'd heard so much about how he was going to kill me, I wasn't interested in talking. Still, Paul went off to talk to him in his cell.

Bitter experience had taught me I needed to make friends and allies fast, so I didn't waste time. Once Paul had gone, I wandered around to see who or what I could find that might be of use. Often in jail, meeting an old friend who owes you, or extracting information from cons about who wants to kill, can be priceless, so I set off on a tour of La Planta.

Just along our corridor, I came across a few white lads, Westerners like us, and I stopped to talk to them: 'Where are you from?'

They eyed me suspiciously and said, '*Russo*. Russia.'

I saw an opportunity. 'Cool, man! Where are you KGB boys staying?'

They liked that and invited me into their cell, where there were also two German lads. We started talking about wars and stuff and I joked with the Germans: 'You can shut up, we fucked you over with Churchill.'

Then the Russians chipped in, adding, 'But you didn't fuck us over. None of you could fuck us.'

These boys were obviously hard as nails, and I was doing everything I could to flatter them and make new allies. 'I'll hold my hands up,' I said. 'I agree. Nobody can do the Russians. You lot are the world's ultimate force. You're the top dogs, and you're clever bastards. I think you could do the Yanks and everything.'

One of the Russians smiled. They'd bought it. He said, 'We Russians, from kids we are taught how to handle a Kalashnikov. If I had my Kalashnikov in here now, I'd let rip with it.'

At that precise moment, Paul walked in with Patrick. There I was, laughing my tits off with these hard-as-fuck Russians, talking about firing assault rifles.

Round one to me.

I ignored Patrick and asked another of the Russians, who'd told me he did tattoos, how much he'd charge to ink me.

At this point, Patrick butted in and said, 'He ain't doing nothing for you. You're going to be a dead corpse tomorrow.'

I knew I had to act fast and I completely fronted him out: 'Patrick, what's the beef with me and you, man?'

Slowly, he said, 'You pulled a knife on me and robbed me.'

'Yeah, well, at the time, why did I do it?' I asked him. 'You weren't giving us fuck all money, you were being a tight bastard, and you were trying to tell me what was what in my prison.'

'You weren't the fucking daddy!' he shouted.

'Yes, I was.' I stared him full in the face, my heart going like the clappers. 'I'd been there longer than you, and we had things running sweet,' I replied. 'If you'd have walked in there before we were there, you'd have been fucked, man. I did you a favour, getting that money off you before one of the head-cases did it. You wouldn't be here now if someone else had mugged you.'

Paul interrupted, 'I told you – Jim was looking out for you and teaching you the right way!'

Patrick looked at me. 'Well, he had a funny fucking way of showing it,' and off he walked, with the hump.

If he was going to do anything, he'd have done it then. It looked like Christian was right: Patrick was all mouth and no bullets.

It was a good result. I'd showed some lads I wasn't prepared to be bullied by Patrick, and I was on a roll. While my stock was high, I told my new Russian pals I was going for a shower – and to look for a good cell.

Despite the fact Patrick seemed to have backed off, I had decided I didn't like being in the cell next to him. He might not have the balls to kill me himself, but he could easily pay some other numpty to do it, and I didn't want to remind him all the time that I was around. Moving seemed to be the only choice I had.

The Russian lad replied: 'You can't do that. You can't just pick a cell.'

'Yes, I can,' I replied, and walked into a cell opposite his that I liked the look of and started having a shower.

The guy whose cell it was, a lad called Charlie, walked in and saw me, saying with disbelief: 'Who's that in my fucking shower?'

I replied calmly, 'I'll talk to you in a minute, I'm showering.'

I think he was so surprised that this bollock-naked English lad was helping himself, he was shocked into submission, and we got chatting.

I told him I was English and in for drug smuggling, and straight away he got who I was: 'Oh, you're that guy from La Vega. Patrick's been on about you,' he said.

I said, 'Good or bad?', and he replied, 'Very bad. Very, very bad. I don't think you're safe here.'

It was obvious the whole prison knew about our beef. 'I'm safe wherever I go, don't worry about it,' I said. 'I'm not dead yet.'

He laughed, and we got talking about who we knew, and I mentioned a guy called Challa Javez I'd known in Yare.

'Challa Javez … the name rings a bell,' Charlie said. 'Oh, yeah, I shot his brother.'

I laughed. 'I think you're on a death list, then, because I'm sure Challa Javez is in La Planta.'

Prisoners always like to brag about who they've done over, and within minutes of meeting Charlie, I'd screwed some priceless information out of him, stuff I could no doubt use to my own advantage. And I was right: Charlie offered to let me stay in his cell if I fed him more info about Challa Javez.

A useful morning's work: I was in Charlie's cell, and I reckoned that I was likely in with Challa Javez, too. And it wasn't long before I found out.

Meanwhile, Paul was doing his best to pour water on Patrick's fire to calm things down and help us find our feet in another new jail. We were back to how we worked best – as a team.

We had heard from Jackie at the Embassy that an old English boy called Bill was serving life for murder in La Planta. After my shower, I tracked him down, and that's how I came to meet an old geezer with a hearing aid, dressed in a safari outfit.

However, he wasn't a particularly nice old geezer. He told me he was born in England but had lived in South Africa, and described how he'd once been so rich, he used to have four servants. 'If those buggers ever stepped out of line, we used to feed them to the lions,' he said. 'It was my land. I did what I wanted.'

With so many black inmates around, I decided I wanted to skip Bill's racist rants, and walked out – straight into the path of Challa Javez.

I immediately saw a good opportunity to dodge our protection fee: this was a guy who wanted my cellmate dead, and if I played it right, it could work out nicely.

Greetings dealt with, I said to him, 'Do you know who's in the cell down the corridor? Charlie, the guy who shot your brother.'

Javez went red with rage immediately. 'What! I'm going to go in there now and slit his throat!'

Once again, I knew his extreme reaction could be turned to my advantage. 'No, leave it for a bit,' I said. 'I think that twat is going to ask me for £100 protection money, but I'm gonna use your name to scare him.' I could see he liked that. 'Leave it with me,' I said. 'You'll get your man, but let me use him first.'

Challa Javez agreed to step down. Even better, he was so grateful to me for helping him find the guy who shot his brother, he offered me the golden ticket I'd been looking for since my arrival at La Planta – access to protection and weapons.

Within the day I was sorted. By trading with the most important prison commodities – information, experience and fear – I'd got a plum cell, a crew willing to bail me out and, most importantly of all, access to a gun if it kicked off with Patrick.

That evening, I heard some lads in the next cell talking, and I was sure I recognised some of the voices as my boys from La Vega. One of them turned out to be Chico, the guy who'd given me advice on my first day at Yare, and who had always backed me up when I was having a beef with someone.

In La Planta, he'd established himself as a major power, one of the top daddies. He'd always been a pretty quiet 'daddy' in Yare, but in La Planta, he had totally flipped, giving him a rep that had earned him top-dog status.

It all started because one of the other daddies, Loco, had approached Chico and told him he wanted to take his place in the hierarchy; but to avoid bloodshed, suggested that Chico could be his right-hand man.

But Chico had said no, so it was agreed it would be sorted via a knife fight. Strict rules of engagement meant that even if Chico had no knife, he would still have to fight – bare-handed. He didn't want to risk his knives being confiscated so, on the day of the duel, Chico had decided to hide all of his weapons in his brother's cell. But his brother fucked up – or stitched him up. When it came time for the knife fight, he didn't bring the weapon.

Chico had had his gun on him, and he had pulled his Glock and shot his brother three times in the face, killing him instantly. He also shot two of his brother's mates through the chest, wasting them.

Chico hadn't given a fuck. He had turned to Loco and said, 'I can't fight you today. My brother fucked up. Let's get it on tomorrow.' His status remained unchallenged.

La Planta was so overcrowded when you looked at it, it was just a sea of arms and heads. We worked out that we had to walk past 300 guns to even get to the canteen every day. I never wanted a Slush Puppy that much!

For that reason, I decided to keep myself to myself in La Planta. I'd had enough of all the violence and killings, and paid an extra £10 a week to have a quieter cell on the same level as the governor's, away from all the nutters. No dickhead would walk down there shooting a gun. It was where I wanted to be. Paul moved to a cell just twenty yards away, too.

Unlike Yare, where you were free to roam, in La Planta we had to spend most days locked up in our cells. I hated the containment, but it kept me out of trouble. I turned my back on the drugs trade going on there, as I knew that if I ever wanted to get free, I had to keep away from violence.

Instead, I turned to weight-training to stay sane. I trained with a few interesting characters. One was a giant Colombian fella called Mesa, who'd murdered a guy he'd suspected was messing around with his wife. He was absolutely massive and looked like he could snap you in half if he ever got hold of you.

There was also a big Dutch guy called Dane, who had murdered a guy in Margarita. We hit it off, as I'm a Manchester United fan and he had a tattoo of a red devil on his arm. Dane had an enormous torso from all the bench presses he'd done with Mesa, but his legs were like toothpicks, a bit like Olive's off *Popeye*. Not that I ever told him that.

We made our own weights out of a scaffolding bar, on the end of which were two car wheels. They weighed in at about 110 kilograms and we used to bench-press them. The wheels were welded on, so you couldn't downgrade. I had to beef up fast: I could do five reps to their ten.

I was definitely calming down, keeping out of trouble. I was quite happy with myself for this, but wondered at the time if there was another reason.

The girls were still allowed to come and visit us, and it was around this time that, for the first time in my life, I couldn't get a hard-on: Siyanni had been for a visit and I hadn't been able to perform. When it happened again a week later, I told a few of the lads about it – and to my astonishment, it had been happening to them, too. We concluded that they were drugging the prison food to keep us quiet. I'd heard of this before, like the rumour about how they used to put bromide in squaddies' tea in World War II to control their sex drives and keep their minds on the game in hand. We all stopped eating the food, and started to prepare our own.

I was speaking to my dad again after the break I'd asked for in Yare, and when I told him, he said, 'You need to get a raw onion, and eat it for breakfast. You'll see, you'll have blue steel.' This sounded about as plausible as farting out of your ear to me, but I tried it, and lo and behold, it worked, although Siyanni moaned about my bad breath!

My new, quieter approach also meant that my war with Patrick fizzled out. Paul had talked to Patrick a lot, and Patrick had decided to drop it all. I owed Paul big time for that. I had been prepared to go to war with Patrick if need be, but Paul had used a more diplomatic approach. Sometimes, even in jail – if you're dealing with the right person – the pen can be mightier than the sword.

By this time, Paul and I had got all our parole paper-work ready. To qualify for release, we had to have a fixed address and a full-time job to go to. Siyanni had agreed to let me move in with her mum, and she'd got me a job in, of all places, a hairdresser's, which she'd arranged because she was a model (she looked like Jennifer Aniston) and knew people in the game. I didn't give a monkey's: I just wanted out. Things, it seemed, were getting better.

Of course, I should never have tempted Fate. Around this time I fell so ill, I thought I was going to die. I'm still not sure if it was food, our living conditions – rats ran around freely – or, more likely, the water. I started with the runs, but it turned into an eight-day session of shitting out blood. It was serious. I'd seen guys die of stomach viruses in Yare and La Vega.

When my stomach lining started coming away, I developed a terrible fever and couldn't even move. I thought my number was up. I'd survived stabbings and avoided bullets – surely a poxy virus wasn't going to take me down?

My fellow cellmates swung into action and dosed me up with their medicine. First, they gave me boiled water poured through porridge oats, which was meant to repair the stomach lining. Another bloke said you had to swallow eight huge balls of bog roll and have a swig of vinegar, but thankfully the Embassy sorted me out with some pills that did the business. I'd lost two stone in a week, but after eleven days of shocking illness, I was finally starting to get better.

I was so glad to be alive. Not only from the virus but, in my weakened state, I'd have been an easy target for an assassin if one had been set on me.

As I pulled through, I started reflecting more on the person I'd become. I realised all these jails had changed me into a Jekyll-&-Hyde-type character. I could be humorous, but then flip into a devil the next minute and be nasty: to survive the shit, I realised, I'd become a shit.

Chucking drugs at the problem to try and make it all go away had seemed like a good idea at the time but, of course, they made me moodier, more paranoid and more temperamental.

El Junquito had shown me that there were nice people in this country, but I knew there were also murderous scum who would stab you for a cigarette. Trying to constantly work out who was what was exhausting.

In Yare, where we were surrounded by crime and guns all the time, I'd even decided it would be a good idea to get out and become a bank robber. I thought it would just be a piece of piss to walk into a joint, scare the fuck out of somebody with a weapon, shout, 'Give me your fucking money!', and leg it. But when we were back to reality again in El Junquito, I realised it was all so stupid. I had got into jail for behaving like that.

I knew it had to end. I couldn't do it any more. We had to step up and focus on our freedom. I'm just glad that we had the shit jails before the good ones. If it had been the other way round, I think we'd still be there. Or, more likely, in a coffin.

I vowed to just get through the last stint of our sentence. I vowed to just get through my time in La

Planta and prayed that a judge would visit us and issue us a pardon. Even though our sentence still officially stood at fifteen years, we both felt that if we put the right paperwork in front of the right judge, then freedom could be ours. I had to look at prison as a school: I'd made mistakes and I had to learn from them. There had been some hard lessons but, unlike many I'd seen fall, I was still breathing. Whereas before I hadn't cared if I'd lived or died, I now realised I wanted to survive. I felt as though I was finally maturing. Crucially, I could see light at the end of the tunnel.

I started softening towards the other cons and, in the holding cell before what turned out to be our final court appearance, actually started talking to other prisoners, in the same way others had showed me that sort of kindness in El Junquito. And it worked. I started getting on with blokes, whereas in Yare I wouldn't even have looked them in the eye for fear of it turning into a knife fight.

Then, finally, the day came when all our release paperwork was signed and correct. Yare had been so isolated, we knew the judges only rarely went there to issue a pardon. But La Planta put us back on the map as judges were more likely to come out there – it was easier to get to, simple as that. But when would our release be agreed, signed and sealed? We had no idea of that, and still were kept totally in the dark.

We were on tenterhooks, praying a judge would come out to La Planta soon. But trouble was brewing, and no judge would come out at a time like that: a couple of National Guards had thrown a grenade into a cell of protesters who'd opened fire on them, and killed eight inmates, and during the next visiting time, thirty-two men from the unit had stormed the police, charged at the open gate and out into the streets of Caracas. They knew the National Guard couldn't open fire on them, as they were surrounded by civilians.

This was the last thing we needed. Surely no judges would come here now? But, in a typically weird twist of Venezuelan justice, it had the opposite effect, and on May 26th, 2000, we heard a judge had finally come to this forgotten hole.

I was having a visit from Siyanni, and we were pretty busy, when Paul ran up and shouted, 'Jim! Quick! A judge is in the prison!' I pulled on my trousers as quickly as I could and ran with Paul to our cells, where we grabbed all our paperwork, then sprinted to the governor's office and joined the queue.

Eventually we were ushered in, and the judge looked over our papers. Behind her on a noticeboard, I saw the names of the thirty-two fugitives who had escaped. Next to eighteen of their names were their fates. The list said things like: 'Dead. Slaughtered. Captured. Drowned. Slaughtered. Caught robbing bank.' I also knew many others would simply vanish, when news of their escape reached their enemies, who would track them down and execute them.

Finally, the judge lowered her glasses and said, 'Your papers all appear to be in order. I can see no reason why you cannot go free today. They will call your name out later. Best of luck in the future. Next!'

Just like that, we were free. It was a pure moment, a complete high – we just couldn't get enough of the excitement. I just remember shouting, 'Wicked! Wicked! WICKED!'

Those last few, fateful hours in La Planta were happy, but sad. I spent a lot of time saying goodbye to my friends. Dane, the big Dutch guy I'd lifted a lot of weights with, said to me, 'Come and see me in Holland some time. I know you will make it back home.' We hugged at that. It meant a lot. Then he broke the ice by saying, 'Now, go and get stuck into all those girls!'

It was against Venezuelan prison rules for a convicted criminal to visit inmates. Even though I would have liked to, I was forbidden from visiting anybody. For the first time in our jail life, we were allowed to pack our stuff and take it with us. As we peeled down our cherished posters of pin-up girls from *Loaded* magazine and my precious Eric Cantona pictures, my heart grew heavy. It felt like I was finally laying my past to rest. Then elation kicked in: we were about to taste freedom for the first time in four years! At 11 p.m., they opened the gates to La Planta, and the first things we saw were Siyanni and Kiki. They each handed us a can of cold lager. Paul and I clanked our cans of beer together and said, 'Cheers, mate. We made it.'

It was the sweetest drink I'd ever tasted in my life.

CHAPTER 11

CITY STREETS

We were kicked out onto the streets of Caracas without a clue of what to expect. Of course, we'd heard plenty of horror stories.

Caracas is Venezuela's capital city and eight million people live there. Modern skyscrapers paid for with oil money are surrounded by sprawling shanty towns that are strewn with garbage, and choked with traffic and stinking pollution.

Away from the posh areas, thieves and vagabonds roamed free. Most of the population seemed to be living on or below the breadline, and with little legitimate work on offer to most, crime was rife. Gangs of men on motorbikes would roar up and mug anybody who looked rich. Guns were everywhere. Certain parts of the city were so dangerous after dark that if you moved faster than a jog, bullets would start spraying in your direction.

The police could do little to maintain order. In Venezuela, it is legal for anybody to carry a gun, so it is considered stupid to take the risk and go without. The week before we got out, a gang of youths on sixteen motorbikes had stormed one of the city's main police stations, and stolen all of the cops' pistols, machine guns and grenades.

The terms of our release meant our ordeal was far from over. Even though we were free, we were both still on parole. That meant that if we screwed up at any time, we'd be back into a maximum-security jail. I had to work every day and sleep in El Junquito jail every weeknight. Only at the weekend was I allowed to stay out. I would have to live like this until 2007.

Paul had worked a clever dodge to avoid having to go back to jail like me, and had played up his earlier tuberculosis record. He knew that if he worked the TB angle, the authorities wouldn't make him go back to clink every night, as they feared he might be contagious or die in their custody. He hooked up with a bent doctor who gave him a sick note every two weeks in exchange for an English lesson. Paul was clever that way. He tried to talk me into doing the same, but I wanted to take my chances back in El Junquito, as I felt it was the one place in Venezuela that had actually helped me. I felt a kinship with other cons and felt I could control my world there. This was incredibly important to me, as the Venezuelan authorities made it crystal clear that if either of us broke the law, we'd be straight back inside La Planta, or even Yare.

At this point, Paul and I went our separate ways for a while. I stayed with Siyanni and her mum. As a model, Siyanni was rich for a Venezuelan, so my life couldn't have been more different. I got on really well with her mum, and had got to know her when she visited Siyanni in La Vega. She was a very spiritual lady, into Zen, yoga, feng shui and astrology. She was a well-known therapist in Caracas and had built up a list of celebrity clients from all over South America.

When we walked into her house on that first night of freedom, Siyanni's mum, who was a smoker, threw me a little pot with weed in it, saying, 'Skin up. You're at peace now.'

I did, and I was. After four years in jail, I might have thought I would have wanted to go out and paint the town red. But I was so physically and emotionally shattered, I went straight to bed.

The job Siyanni had got me – washing hair in a salon – was fine, and I was grateful for the work. But I thought it was a bit gay, too, so I pleaded with her to let me do maintenance work around the salon instead. That all changed when I went in for my first day.

The salon was top-notch, in an affluent area of Caracas called Las Mercedes. And the women were absolutely gorgeous! All the top soap stars and models went there. Not soon after I started, a Mexican babe called Eleanor Bad – gorgeous, big brown eyes – walked in, who I recognised as a massive soap star. I had to wash her hair, and could barely contain myself. I even washed Miss Universe's hair, too.

As a *gringo*, I had novelty value, and many of the girls flirted like mad. Latin girls are naturally very flirtatious and sexually charged, which posed its own set of constant temptations. One time, a girl whose hair I was washing stood up, bent over, pulled up her mini skirt and flashed me her yellow thong, saying, 'You want this for dinner?' She had the perfect Latin, carnival arse. I had to cross my legs and throw iced water in my face, but I resisted.

After all those years in savage jails hanging out with killers and drug addicts, I had to pinch myself that this was actually happening to me. I was living with the super-rich and high class – it felt like I'd gone from a temple for Shaolin monks to something out of this world. I was making £15 a day, which was like making £150 a day in England. Siyanni's mum had given me a car. Sometimes, my new life seemed more surreal than jail. It was totally mad, and I could not believe my luck.

I worked in the salon for about three months, and started getting the hang of the outside world again. It was a good time, but it meant that going back to El Junquito, to sleep in a prison cell every weeknight, was beginning to get difficult and depressing. I had a taste of freedom, but come 8 p.m., I had to be in a cell with five other inmates who were all on parole, too, kipping on a bunk bed next to a piss bucket. My life was totally schizophrenic. Every evening I had to go and see the governor, salute him, at which he'd say, 'Have you been a good boy today?', and I'd have to reply, 'Yes, sir, I've been a very good boy. I've been working all day and not broken the law once.' Then he'd check his paperwork and say, 'Well, I can't see there have been any complaints about you. So, go to your cell and see you tomorrow.' It was incredibly patronising; I was being treated like a child, a moron – or both.

I really struggled with this daily loss of liberty. My freedom felt fragile, especially as the stress of it all turned me to drugs again. Going from the streets to a dungeon every night, and staying sober, just wasn't an option. To cope with the depressing approach of lockdown, I would neck a bottle of Pernod, score some drugs and traipse across town to jail. I hid rocks of crack between my toes, or taped weed to my balls, as the searches they gave you were only ever half-arsed; no more than going into a nightclub. I knew it was breaking the terms of my bail, but I kind of didn't care. I was, by now, really down again.

The shit really hit the fan after some idiot started bringing a knife into El Junquito every night. The guards raided our cell and found it.

'If this happens again, then all sixty of you are going back to a maximum-security prison!' bellowed the guard. His message was brutally clear: if one person screwed up, at any time, we were *all* going down.

I was furious and squared up to this fat, toad-faced bastard – who amazingly was called Malacucho, just like my nemesis in Yare – and told him I wasn't going to stand for him coming into jail tooled up.

'Fuck you, pinky!' he shouted, but he soon backed down when he found out I'd spent years in La Vega and Yare without getting killed. My reputation made him back off – for now.

One night soon after, however, he stashed his knife under my mattress while I slept 'for a laugh' and I knew I couldn't stand any more of this stress. Without breaking a single law myself, I could be back to square one. And, as a second-time offender who had broken parole, I'd be looking at a ten-year sentence. I'd be right back where I started. I would have rather died than go back to Yare, and I knew Paul fully agreed.

The terms of our liberty were extremely fragile. Out on the streets, we were breaking the law·all the time, without even trying. Under the strict terms of our bail, it was almost impossible not to fall foul of the law: Paul liked a flutter on the gee-gees, and even gambling on a horse race was a breach of his bail. I was driving a car without insurance and hanging out with people who carried guns – more or less everybody you met in Caracas – which was behaviour that could see me get slammed up again. Even shooting off a few rounds at the shooting range next to Siyanni's flat was illegal.

Worse, as *gringos*, we were magnets for corrupt cops, who kept shaking us down for bribes. Bent police were actively targeting us almost every time we went out. It just seemed that at every turn, the odds of making a go of it and going straight were stacked against us. One time I was given a false $100 bill as change in a night-club, and had to pay off a cop (with pukka cash), who just happened to tap me on the shoulder at that precise moment. Another time I fell asleep while drunk in a bar and was woken by a pistol tapping me on the head. Only a hefty cash bribe to the National Guard had kept me out of La Vega's drunk tank, where I'd have been sentenced to the full ten years again.

Prostitutes, too, were everywhere in the bars of Caracas, and would flock around us, only to try and pick our pockets. When we tried to stop them, burly security guards who were all in on the scam would pile in with shotguns, and threaten to call the cops unless we gave them all our money. It was a nightmare. Every time we went out for a quiet drink, it ended up like going into a bar in the Wild West.

If I had got caught with even a spliff, I'd have been straight back to Yare. Yet everywhere I went, drugs were in my face. One day I saw a National Guard throw a spliff in front of an American tourist in the street, then throw him in a van on the strength of it. I felt sorry for the bloke – he'd fallen foul of the age-old trick the guards used to pull inside jails. He'd be looking at twenty-five years unless he could pay his way out.

I decided I needed to escape Caracas and its constant danger, and contacted my old friend from Yare, Al Kemid, who'd been released and now lived in the countryside. But when he came to pick me up, and I went to put my stuff in the boot of his car, I saw in there an almighty pile of shotguns, grenades and handguns, all in a big bag, stacked up to the hilt.

He told me that he was worried that the two men he'd murdered for robbing his brother's shop might send people after him for revenge, so he had to be tooled up at all times. 'If those motherfuckers come after me, I'm going down guns blazing,' he told me. But if Al Kemid was stopped by the cops at any point, and his boot searched – a routine occurrence in Caracas – I'd be straight back to jail.

I suddenly realised with cold clarity that this could happen to me or Paul at any time. We were heading for certain disaster, and I knew right then that I could not carry on living like this.

As a tall, red-haired *gringo* working in the hair salon, I stood out, and was spotted by a model scout. I worked with Venezuela's top weather girl, who I'd watched on

TV in jail. I was also offered a Coca-Cola campaign in Brazil, but didn't have a passport, and wasn't allowed to leave the country, anyway. I'd have got £3,000 for that, and not being able to do it put me on a right downer.

Not long after, I was moaning about it in a bar to a friend of mine called Jose, whose wife worked at the airport. Jose said, 'You want a fake passport? I can sort one out for you, *no problemo*. I have a contact, an expert, who can help. But he's not cheap. It'll be £500 per document.' At that point, a light bulb went on in my head. Could this be our way out of Venezuela? It was, after all, a country with no extradition agreement with the UK.

Our full, genuine passports were being held by the British Embassy, but we were not allowed them until 2007, which was still over six years away, and there was just no way on earth we'd be able to stay out of trouble until then. I knew this was dodgy as hell, but what was the alternative? We were free, but still prisoners. OK, if we got nicked using the passports, we'd get banged up again. But that was on the cards anyway. And if we made it back to Blighty and were collared, they'd lock us up on British soil, but so what? I knew that had to be better than Yare or La Planta.

I contacted Paul and told him what was going on. It turned out he'd been thinking of an angle to leg it from the country, too. It's a legal requirement in Venezuela to carry photo ID at all times but, as non-nationals, we didn't qualify for an ID card. Yet nor would the government allow the British Embassy to release our passports. Paul was living forty yards from a beach with Kiki's mum, and made a good living selling cold beers to surfers. But the cops picked him out all the time: with no ID, they could lock him up at any point, and bribes were taking most of his earnings. Like me, he was in a catch-22 situation.

Escaping Venezuela on false passports? We were damned if we did and damned if we didn't try.

Paul had pleaded with the Embassy to give him his passport back so that he could avoid the police hassle, and at this point they got in touch and issued him with a temporary passport.

At that moment, it felt as though all the planets had lined up. I had a false passport teed up, and Paul had a legitimate temporary one. But could we make it back home?

We decided it was time to get out of this mess, if it was the last thing we ever did, but it was a huge gamble.

Then I got the phone call that told me my fake passport would be with me in two weeks' time. I finally decided it was time to get out, before I was either jailed or killed. It was time to go home. After six months of living on a knife edge, I phoned Paul and we both decided we had to go. We'd have to leave Siyanni and Kiki behind, but it was time to get back to normality.

*

Everything started happening very quickly. Things were getting properly dodgy inside El Junquito every weeknight. The economic situation in Venezuela was getting worse, so the guys I shared a cell with had increasingly been turning to street crimes and robbery to stay alive. But that made them marked men, so some lads had started bringing guns into the jail to protect themselves – being around them was a disaster waiting to happen. One wrong slip from any of them and I'd be back in Yare faster than you could say, 'Screw you, *gringo*.'

I was already on my last warning at El Junquito for getting back to jail late after partying. With my fake passport lined up, I couldn't risk something going wrong now, so decided it was worth taking the dangerous and illegal step of breaking the conditions of my bail – I stopped reporting to El Junquito to sleep.

But where could I stay? I'd split with Siyanni after telling her I was going home, and couldn't go near Paul's apartment as the cops would surely be watching it now I was a wanted fugitive. Worse, I'd run out of money and my dad couldn't wire any to me for a week.

With nowhere else to go, I slept under a bridge for a while with other down-and-outs, just trying to disappear. The tramps kept trying to steal my shoes as I slept but worse, the police would often come and move us on.

I had to get out of the areas the cops knew I frequented. Where would be the last place on earth the police would look for me? I decided to sleep by the bins in the car park underneath Pettihota – the Scotland Yard of Caracas.

I'd studied the police's comings and goings for eight days solid, and knew exactly when the shifts changed and when the safe times were. I was working on the logic of what wanted fugitive would be mad enough to walk right into the lion's den like that? One who thought one step ahead, I hoped. I was desperate, and broke, and once again, it was all about pure survival.

My dodgy passport was still waiting for its stamp to show I'd entered the country legitimately. I called Jose every day to find out any news and, at last, Jose arranged it via a bribed airport worker. I finally got the passport.

It was a brilliant forgery, complete with my photo and a legitimate stamp. My spirits soared. I was one step nearer freedom, if only I could just evade the cops for a few more days.

At this point, my dad flew to Caracas to hand over my ticket money to me. He insisted on doing it in person after all that had happened: 'I'm leaving nothing to chance, son. We're going to get you home.' I moved into his hotel with him after a week of sleeping rough and, feeling on top of the world, went to buy my ticket home.

On the way to the travel agent, however, I had the biggest fright. Rounding a corner, I looked up to see two National Guards walking straight towards me. I was on

Venezuela's wanted list; I was a tall, ginger *gringo* – and they looked straight through me.

Once I had stopped sweating, I went into the travel agents and bought a one-way ticket to England, via Colombia, on the next available flight out, in one week's time. I was so nearly home.

With my dad in town, we met up with Paul to discuss our best strategy of getting safely back to the UK.

We all agreed it would be suicide to try and make it back together. We'd stand out too much – I was on the run from the police and there was a directive out for my arrest, so we decided to go our separate ways.

Paul was to go first even though it meant leaving his beloved Kiki.

He reasoned it would be better to fly from Colombia, and took a coach into the neighbouring country. On the way in, there was no security whatsoever, and he got waved straight over the border. Paul phoned his mum from Cucuta, just over the border, and told her where he was. She went mad with him for blowing his parole conditions, but agreed to send him money for his air fare home. But when he went to the Western Union to collect the money, they would not accept his passport as ID because it hadn't been stamped on the way into Colombia. To have any chance of getting home, Paul had to run the gauntlet again and go back into Venezuela to pass back through Customs to get the stamp he needed. It was agony upon agony for the poor bloke, but he did it. Back at the Western Union, they finally gave Paul his £1,600, but as it was in local currency, the wad of dough was ten inches thick. Being seen with that kind of brass on the streets of Cucuta was a death sentence, so he had to stuff it down his shorts, up his T-shirt, anywhere to conceal it. But he made it to a travel agent and booked the next available flight to Heathrow.

Paul had made it out of Venezuela, and now all I had to do was make it through one more week in Caracas.

My dad was holed up in a hotel, and I'd hired a bodyguard for him: I didn't want to take any chances with his safety. We just needed to lie low and chill in the hotel, but after a day of that I got cabin fever and really needed something to help me calm down. I decided to pop out to score some weed from a friend I had in the neighbourhood.

I had done the deal and was on my way back to the hotel when I walked into an open courtyard, like a basketball court, between some tower blocks. Well, there were two motorbike cops there and they'd lined about thirty locals up against the wall, giving them a heavy shakedown. One of the cops looked the works: mirrored shades, half-motorcycle helmet like a German army piss-pot, obviously ready to crack jaws.

One of the boys he was searching I knew, and he flashed me a glance. Straight away this copper clocked it. He pistol-whipped the boy to the ground, splitting his head like a watermelon and sending blood every-where, then pointed his gun at me and shouted, 'You! Stay there!'

This was a serious situation. I'd got weed on me – it had only cost me £5 but it was a big size, about the size of a ten-pack of fags, all compressed in a block. It was definitely enough to send me down, and it wasn't even hidden – it was in a cigarette packet in my shorts' pocket. With this cop's eyes on me, there was no way I could try and conceal or dump it without his seeing.

I was just thinking, 'My dad's in the hotel. I'm going tomorrow. I'm free. And now I'm fucked and I'm going straight back to jail.' I seriously considered running, but knew he'd have shot me in the back.

The copper walked over, and shouted, 'You! Shoes off and up against the wall!'

Even though I knew what he was saying, I pulled the dumb *gringo* routine, and said, 'Huh? No speak Spanish. I'm a tourist.'

He pointed his gun at my feet and shouted in English, 'Shoes!'

I pulled off my trainers, he checked them for stash, then started frisking me down. I saw my whole life flash before me: this was the end. Should I go for his gun and just take him out? For a split second I consid-ered it. I really do think at that point I'd have rather gone down fighting, or even died, than go back to prison in Venezuela.

The copper slipped his hand in my pocket, felt the packet of fags with the weed in it – and just left it there. He stepped away, and said, 'OK. Go!'

I felt blessed, like nothing could come between me and sweet freedom now. I got back to the hotel and told my dad, and he said, 'Right, you're not leaving this hotel again, son. Please don't screw this up.' It was some serious shit for us both.

The next day, and we were off to the airport. I checked in on the flight to Colombia with no problems, but I was absolutely terrified of walking down the tunnel that led to the plane. The thought of it brought back terrible flashbacks, awful memories of being nicked four years ago, and it felt like facing my worst and most terrifying innermost fears.

I was shitting it. What if somebody recognised me from before?

At that moment, a party of people starting walking towards me. Unbelievably, Jackie from the British Embassy was among them. I yanked a newspaper up in front of my face; my heart was hammering out of my chest. 'Please don't see me.' They walked straight past me, laughing and joking among themselves.

I didn't want to focus on that tunnel. But it had to be walked.

Halfway down, I bumped into a girl I'd done some modelling with. She was Colombian and was going home to Bogata. After my initial fright at seeing her, I got chatting with her, and completely forgot about the tunnel. Once again, it seemed like destiny, and I breezed on to the plane.

Seated on the plane, I put my headphones on. Just as we took off, U2's *Beautiful Day* started. We were flying over a beach, seeing people down there, the coast, the houses, the jungle. It was exactly the same sight I'd seen four years ago on my way in; a sight I'd often thought I'd never see again. The tears welled up in my eyes, and I thought, 'It is a beautiful day and I'm going home. It's all over.'

Only it wasn't – not yet. We landed in Bogota after three hours, and I started shitting myself, because it's a notoriously hard country to get out of due to its drug connections. All I kept thinking about was *Scarface*, gangsters and the murderous drug cartel leader, Pablo Escobar. I feared security would be tight as a duck's arse.

But my fear disappeared as I rounded a corner and, through a glass wall, saw a hand poking out from around the corner. I thought, 'I recognise those hands, those rings … fuck me, it's Paul Loseby!'

I started running. Paul saw me; he jumped up and we just embraced. Two lost brothers reunited. We made our way over to the bar. 'I think it's your round, kid,' I joked.

We raised a beer to each other and smiled. We didn't even have to talk. Just being there, safe and together, said it all.

Without even knowing, we'd booked on the same flight back to England. This was more than pure coincidence. This was divine intervention. We were too elated to even worry about it increasing our chances of getting nicked and we were over the border, in a whole different country now.

We sat together on the flight home, and once again sang Oasis tunes as we drank the bar dry.

As we belted out *Champagne Supernova* again, people were giving us funny looks, like we were two English thugs on the rampage, but we just didn't care.

We were alive. We'd made it home.

EPILOGUE

PAUL LOSEBY

I'll never forget the moment when I made it through UK Customs and finally got back onto British soil. I kneeled down and kissed the ground, like the Pope. It was the sweetest moment of my life. Liberty was finally mine.

However, because I was only on a temporary visa, I was taken to an interview room and for forty-five gruelling minutes they shot the same questions at me: 'Why do you have a temporary passport? Where's your full passport? Where are you going to live? How much money do you have?' It was merciless, and finally I lost my temper.

I expected to get led off to jail, but instead they looked at me, stamped my passport and said, 'Welcome to the United Kingdom, Mr Loseby. You're free to go.' Those words meant everything to me.

I walked through the gate and my precious mum, Wendy, was waiting there, the most important person in the entire world. She'd been there for me through thick and thin, and I just became a little boy again. All that shit we'd been through over there, all that hard-man bull-shit – the guns, the person I'd had to become – it was all irrelevant. I hugged her, and just kept saying, 'Mum, I'm so sorry. I'm so sorry.' And she did what any proper mum would do – she gave me a good, old-fashioned clip round the ear, and said, 'No need to say sorry, duck. You're my son and I love you.' She put everything to one side and gave me unconditional love. I finally got to see my dad, Graham, too. It was all so, so humbling.

It made life worth living again. My self-esteem was at rock bottom, but that one moment meant that every gruelling day in Venezuela, when my life hadn't even seemed worth two shits, had been worth it. I just got that child-like feeling where you want your head to be stroked and to be told everything is going to be all right.

I also had the most overwhelming sense of relief and pride in being British. This was my England, my coun-try, a land I thought I'd never see again. I felt like a returning soldier. It was totally mind-blowing.

I went back to my mum's house, and hid away from the world. I found out, however, that when Jim and I were a fortnight late getting back from Venezuela, the Russ-ian had smashed his way into a friend of mine's flat, held a sawn-off shotgun to his head and screamed, 'Where the fuck are those two thieving cunts? Tell me or I will blow your fucking brains out!' He thought we'd done a runner with his ten kilos of drugs, and had only believed my friend didn't know anything about it when he was crying in a heap on the floor. It made me angry, but it clicked into place that the Russian hadn't grassed us up, after all. He thought we'd ripped him off and tried to vanish with the profits. When he'd found out we were locked up, he'd vanished himself, for fear of retribution.

Getting back into the real world wasn't easy. For three weeks I didn't leave the house, but then the local paper, the *Leicester Mercury*, found out I was back and came to my doorstep and printed that I was free and back home. I understand it was a big local interest story – we'd had Labour MP for Leicester East, Keith Vaz, petitioning our story in Parliament all the time we'd been away – but it meant that I then got recognised everywhere I went.

One day in the queue at the local supermarket, a woman pointed me out to her daughter and said, 'There's that twat, the drug smuggler,' and it made me so angry. But I'd been through cognitive behavioural therapy, which helped me to rethink how I thought and acted, and I had learned to press the pause button and think before I spoke. But I still went and fronted her out, saying, 'Excuse me, I heard what you said. But you don't know me. I'm not that person any more. I've done my time. I've changed.'

When she spat in my face and said, 'Oh, fuck off!', I wondered then if I'd ever escape my past.

Some months later, James and I did a TV documentary for *Banged Up Abroad* and I saw my face in all the TV mags in Asda. We were in the surreal position of being 'Pick of the Week' in all of them.

I wanted to do that show. I wanted to let the world know that drug smuggling was for mugs and just wasn't worth it. But it also gave me a notoriety I didn't want. Kids on the street stopped me, asked for my autograph and treated me like I was a gangster. I made sure that when I talked to these kids on the estate, they didn't get what they bargained for. Instead of me bigging it up like they expected, I told them crime was for mugs, and jails are shite. If one less person ends up in clink because of what I've been through and the story I've told, I'll be happy. I don't want sympathy. I just want to move on.

I wanted a quiet life so moved to a small village away from my estate. I just wanted to vanish. I couldn't stand constantly being judged by strangers. What gave them the right? I also wanted a trade, a normal life after all those years of madness, so trained as a carpenter for Leicester City Council. It was tough going back to college at twenty-seven – it was full of kids a decade younger than me, but I cracked on, did well and got a full-time job.

But then one day at work, I looked down at a red drill box, and instead of it I saw a giant pool of blood – I was having the most terrible flashback to the time that poor guy had his brains blown out in the dinner queue early on in our time in Yare. Totally incapacitated, I had to go home. I knew then that I hadn't dealt with all the stuff. I'd tried my best, but this shit could not just be swept under the carpet.

I sought professional help, and was diagnosed with post-traumatic stress disorder, like squaddies get from being in war zones. It was a relief to know I wasn't just imagining it. With treatment, there was hope in sight.

I'll always regret that things didn't work out with Kiki, but I'm now a proud dad of four kids. It gives me a sense of future, of life. I named my second nipper James, after my brother, Jim Miles. I've never had a real brother, but Jim is one to me. No matter what we've been through, I will love that guy like a brother until the day I die. He watched my back. I watched his. We were *compadres*. We would not have made it without each other.

I know just what I'd say to Paul Loseby aged twenty-one, if I sat next to him in a pub. I'd say, 'Don't waste your life, kid. What's £9,000 for drug smuggling in a lifetime? Don't fuck it up. Be a good son, lead a normal life. Crime, it's for idiots.' But I don't think he would have listened. I was just another cocksure kid who never thought of the consequences of his actions. You see people like I was then everywhere on the streets of Britain, every single day. I don't want them to screw up like I did.

But, against overwhelming odds, I think I've emerged from this a stronger person. I can speak fluent Spanish, and plan to train as a translator one day. In Yare, Luis also taught me to be an expert tattooist. I came back with skills I'd never have got otherwise. Jail taught me more than anything else that you need to adapt to survive.

Telling this story again has been very therapeutic, and it's helped me to make sense out of all that madness. But I'd like it to end soon. Back then, I often wanted to die. Now, I want to live. I want to be normal. And, most of all, I just want to forget.

JAMES MILES

To this day, I still have nightmares about my time in those Venezuelan jails.

It's always the same scenes. In one, I'm going along in a car with my girlfriend, when I become aware we're being chased by some dark, unseen force into a multi-storey car park. Once inside, the shutters go down, locking us in. Inside, it's full of baying Venezuelans, and suddenly I'm tied to a chair, I can't move and they start saying they're going to rape my girlfriend. There's nothing I can do to stop it. I wake up in a blind panic every time, my sheets drenched with sweat.

Other times, it's dreams of giant, greasy rodents eating me alive. They're crawling all over me and nibbling my face off, and I'll sit bolt upright. Only, I'm not in bed with my girlfriend in Leicester, I'm still back there in Yare.

Or I'm in a room with really high walls, and the only exit is right at the top of those walls, but there's no ladder, and I'm scratching at the walls trying to climb, but can't.

I know I'm having flashbacks to Yare. It's like all the worst experiences we went through, all rolled into one terrifying, inescapable memory.

At first I couldn't bring myself to explain them to my friends or my parents. Nothing like that had even happened to me, and I didn't understand why I was thinking this shit.

I decided to seek help, and went to see a psychotherapist called John Monk-Steel, who specialises in trauma and abuse counselling. His practice was based in an old, Victorian house with high ceilings, leather chairs and an open fire. It was *tranquilo* – peaceful – and really nice. It was, finally, a place I felt comfortable in and could open up.

They were gruesome sessions. John wanted to open the darkest doors of my mind and look behind them. It really helped, and for a time I would think I'd been cured. Then I'd have another flashback, and start wondering again if this nightmare, these feelings of enforced containment, would ever end.

The real world was confusing to me, too. I had no idea what to expect from Dad or my mum, Georgina, and I found Leicester totally disorientating. When I'd landed back in Britain, I'd found my mum waiting for me. Squeezing her tiny body tight, I'd felt so happy. But I knew I wasn't her little boy any more. When I had left for Venezuela, I had known everybody on my road. Now, I didn't know anyone more than the occasional face I'd recognise in the street. And I couldn't believe how multi-cultural Leicester had become. It was like I'd returned to a different world.

I didn't recognise my youngest brother, Craig, at a family reunion. He'd had big, baby eyes with his hair in a basin cut when I'd last seen him as a kid. Now he was a grown man. I just thought, 'How did that happen?' It scared and upset me. I realised I'd never get those lost years back.

To cope out there, to survive, I'd deleted the English way of life from my mind and become Venezuelan. When I got back, I expected to be able to pick up where I left off. But everything had totally changed. It felt like every-body had moved on in life except me. It completely messed me up.

*

We got loads of hate mail on YouTube when we did *Banged Up Abroad*. A lad from Brooklyn, New York, wrote, 'You two are pussy ho's, get your asses to Brooklyn and get really busted up.' It was pathetic, the way people from all over the world, who didn't know us, were just chucking abuse. I think it really wound Paul up, but I said to him, 'So what? Don't reply to them or you'll just give them something to build on.'

I was finally trying to turn the other cheek and not let my temper control my actions. I told my counsellor that I didn't want to fly off the handle any more. The person I'd become in Venezuela would reach out and eliminate people for saying nasty things. Here, people would wind me up and if I saw something metal sitting there, my inner animal wanted to reach over and use it as a weapon on them.

I had been really paranoid in jail, and didn't have a conscience there. I only regretted things after the damage was done. And those problems didn't magically vanish when liberty was finally mine and I got back to England.

Sadly, life's not as simple or easy as that.

And it didn't get simpler. People from my past kept approaching me, asking if I wanted to get involved in crime again. They were talking about stick-ups at post offices and banks, and thought I'd be up for it as I'd handled so many guns in jail. Other people offered to pay me to do people over – 'vigilante work' they called it. I couldn't escape the dark side of Jim Miles.

Gradually, the psychotherapy helped me to stop having nightmares, but it didn't help curb my temper, or mood swings.

Then, thirteen months after I got back to Britain, I became a dad to my little boy.

I was there at the birth. It was an intense and very emotional fourteen-hour labour. Nothing was happening – he needed to come out; they thought he was going to die. They told me they needed to use forceps to get him out, and I just broke down in tears. But he made it. And after that, whenever I thought Venezuela was bad, I realised my baby dying would have been far worse. It made me realise life wasn't just about me any more.

Seamus is everything to me. Every time I think about going back to the old Jim, I have to remember that.

My head virtually screwed itself on overnight.

I took on a serious job, took driving lessons and started saving money so my girlfriend and kid didn't have to live in a council house. Now I work six days a week in Traffic Management on the North Circular Road in London, then drive back to Leicester to be with my missus and Seamus. I pay taxes. I'm a normal member of society and it feels good to be normal. And I never thought I'd say that.

I have to look at the positives. My dad once said to me, 'If you hadn't gone to Venezuela, you'd probably be doing a life sentence here, anyway. Nobody could tell you anything when you were eighteen.' He was right. I had been on a terrible, self-destructive course.

Venezuela was like a school for me where I finally learned my lesson. People died out there, but it was nearly always for a reason. They'd been bad. They paid for it. Their lives weren't good lives. They were some shithead who would go on to cause misery and do something bad anyway. Is the world a poorer place without them? No. That is what helps me get through the night.

I've always thought, 'The bad things in life taste good, and the good things taste bad.' Crime tasted good at the time, but it was shit after. And I mean really, genuinely and sincerely *shit*. It's just not worth the pain, both for you or your loved ones.

Likewise, the desperate things I witnessed tasted sour back then, but they've made me a better person now. I've seen good men die young. Sons, fathers. I don't want to be one of them. Life can be shit, but you have to take it on if you ever hope to get stronger.

Many of my great friends in Venezuela ended up dead, God rest their souls. The ones I got really close to, they always said to me, 'Don't be like a snake. Windy roads lead to bad trouble.' They had a phrase for it: *Todo polante*. 'Everything forward.' That's my path now. Always forward.

*

So, in a strange way, all the brutality and shit I went through out there saved my life. Now, it's about the new life of my son. Unlike me, he can take a good path. Hopefully, I've fucked up so he'll never have to. I hope for whatever he hopes for. He is nine years old now, and I know he'll read this book one day. I want him to be proud of the man I am now, not the shit I was then. That's why I wanted to tell my tale, to do it justice. It wasn't an easy story to tell. But it was my story.

ACKNOWLEDGEMENTS

We would like to thank: Paul's mum Wendy and his beautiful children who he loves dearly; Jim's mum and dad; Josefina; Tony Roe; the British Embassy and everybody else who helped us during and after Venezuela. We are also grateful to those who helped us tell our story – Ben Barrett at Raw TV, our editor Kelly Ellis and Martin Daubney.